ANNE GEDDES

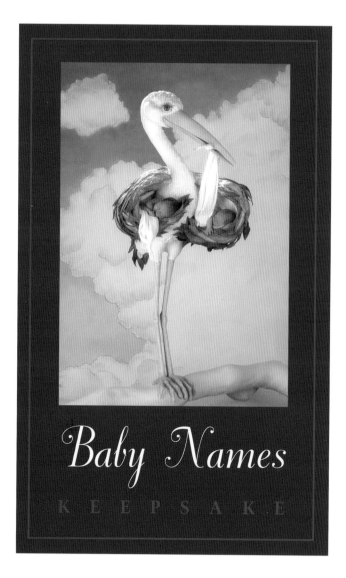

Baby Names

ANNE GEDDES ™

ISBN 0-7683-2001-1

© Anne Geddes 1997
Anne Geddes is the registered trademark of The Especially Kids Company Limited.

Published in 1997 by Cedco Publishing Company,
2955 Kerner Blvd, San Rafael, CA 94901

First USA Edition, May 1997
Fourth Printing, August 1997

Designed by Frances Young
Produced by Kel Geddes
Color separations by Image Centre

Printed through Midas Printing Limited, Hong Kong

Please write to us for a FREE FULL COLOR catalog of our fine Anne Geddes
calendars and books, Cedco Publishing Company, 2955 Kerner Blvd.,
San Rafael, CA 94901.
Visit our website : www.cedco.com

I am very fortunate that through my work I am able to be in contact with many new babies, with names ranging from the traditional to more unusual choices.

The naming of your new baby should be fun and exciting, and I have endeavoured to include many names in this book that you may not have considered before.

But this book is also meant to become a cherished family heirloom, with an individual record of every baby's naming details, to be handed down throughout the family and eventually become a fascinating family record for future generations to enjoy.

Baby Names Keepsake

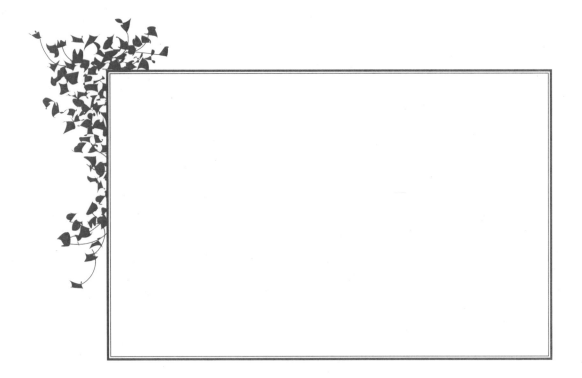

$\mathcal{N}$ame
....

$\mathcal{D}$ate of birth
....

$\mathcal{P}$arents
....

$\mathcal{W}$hy your name was chosen
....

....

$\mathcal{O}$ther names considered
....

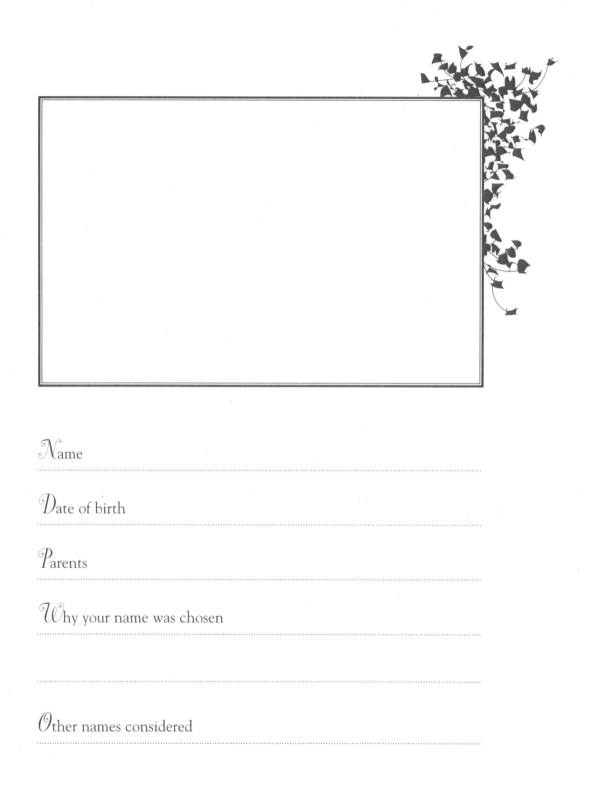

$\mathcal{N}$ame

....

$\mathcal{D}$ate of birth

....

$\mathcal{P}$arents

....

$\mathcal{W}$hy your name was chosen

....

....

$\mathcal{O}$ther names considered

....

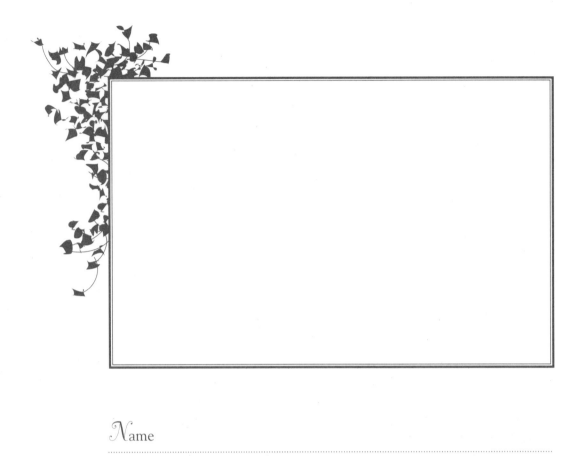

Name
....

Date of birth
....

Parents
....

Why your name was chosen
....

....

Other names considered
....

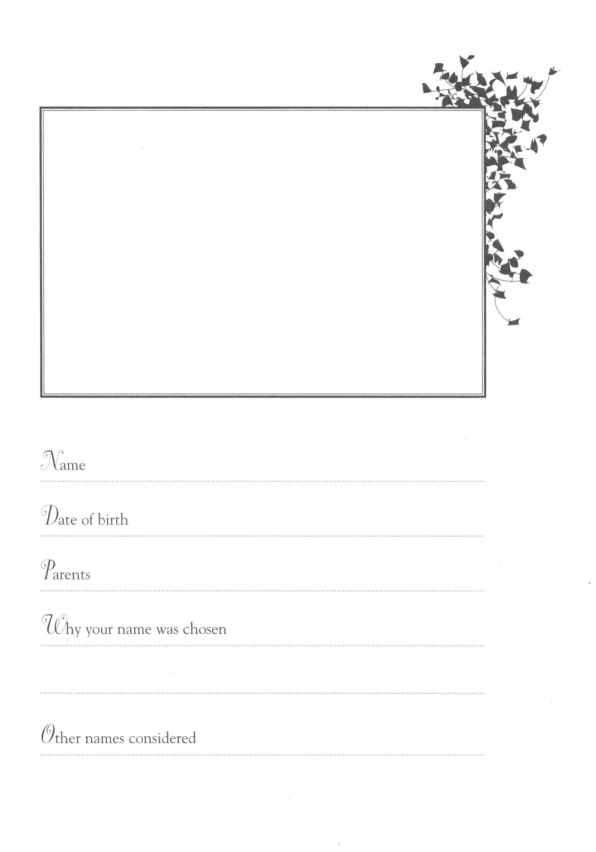

*N*ame

....

*D*ate of birth

....

*P*arents

....

*W*hy your name was chosen

....

....

*O*ther names considered

....

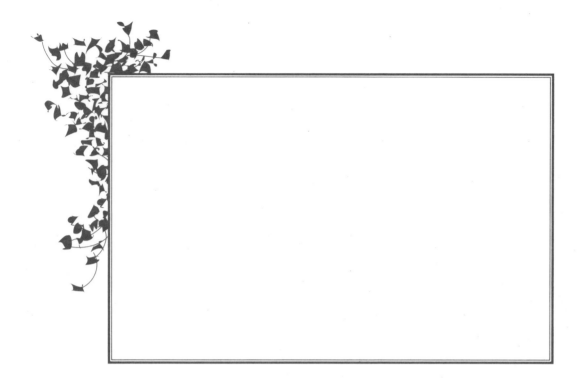

$\mathcal{N}$ame

....

$\mathcal{D}$ate of birth

....

$\mathcal{P}$arents

....

$\mathcal{W}$hy your name was chosen

....

....

$\mathcal{O}$ther names considered

....

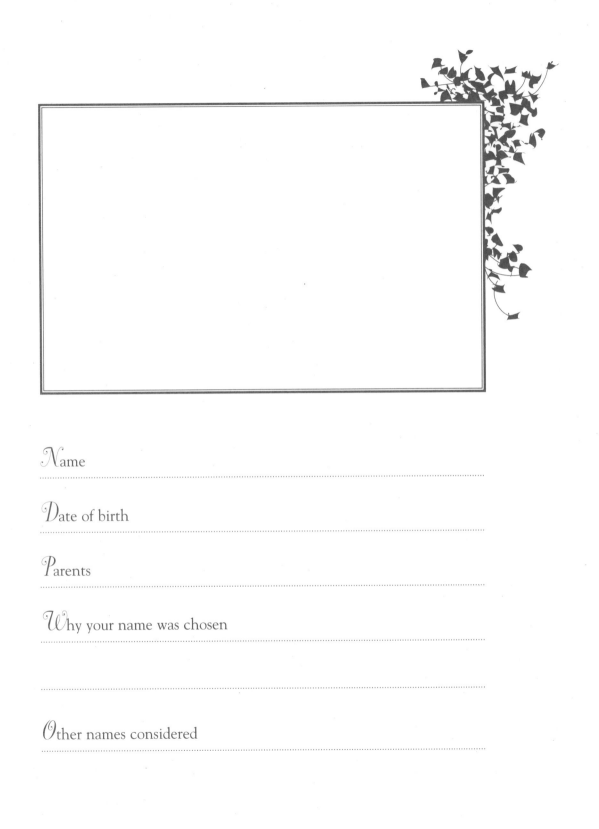

Name
....

Date of birth
....

Parents
....

Why your name was chosen
....

....

Other names considered
....

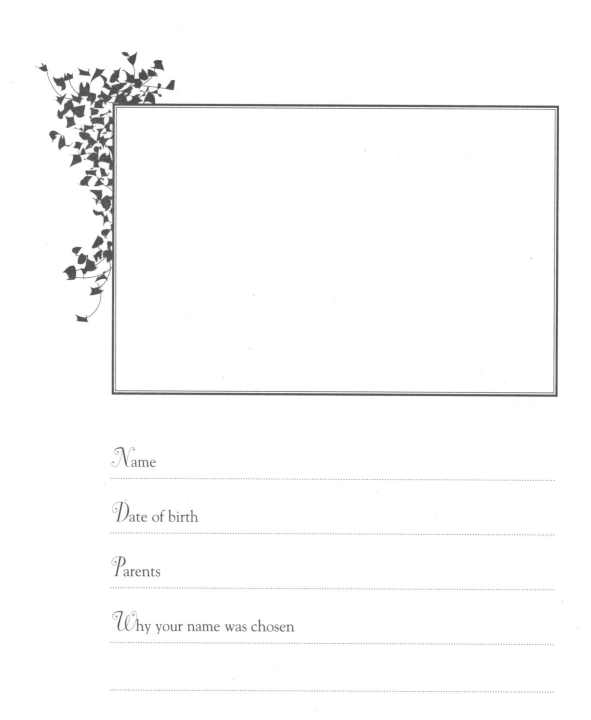

$\mathcal{N}$ame
....

$\mathcal{D}$ate of birth
....

$\mathcal{P}$arents
....

$\mathcal{W}$hy your name was chosen
....

....

$\mathcal{O}$ther names considered
....

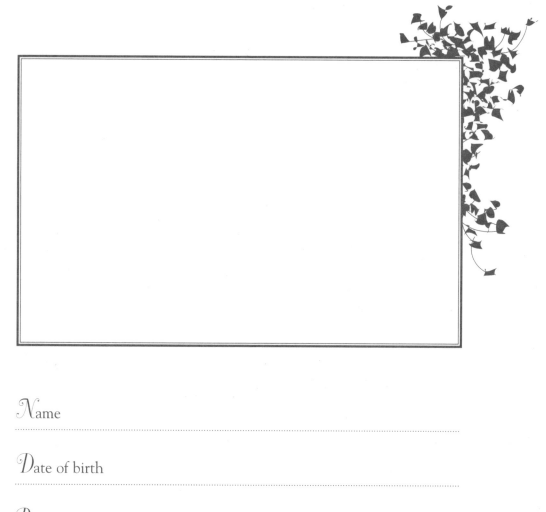

$\mathscr{N}$ame

....

$\mathscr{D}$ate of birth

....

$\mathscr{P}$arents

....

$\mathscr{W}$hy your name was chosen

....

....

$\mathscr{O}$ther names considered

....

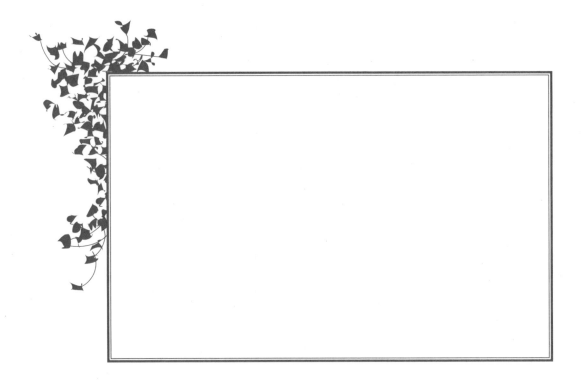

$\mathcal{N}$ame

. . . .

$\mathcal{D}$ate of birth

. . . .

$\mathcal{P}$arents

. . . .

$\mathcal{W}$hy your name was chosen

. . . .

. . . .

$\mathcal{O}$ther names considered

. . . .

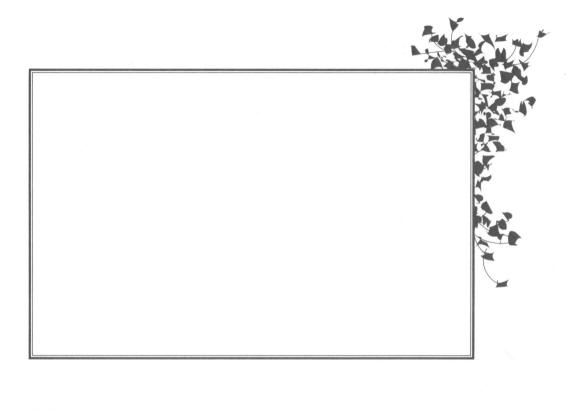

$\mathcal{N}$ame

. . . .

$\mathcal{D}$ate of birth

. . . .

$\mathcal{P}$arents

. . . .

$\mathcal{W}$hy your name was chosen

. . . .

. . . .

$\mathcal{O}$ther names considered

. . . .

*N*ame

....

*D*ate of birth

....

*P*arents

....

*W*hy your name was chosen

....

....

*O*ther names considered

....

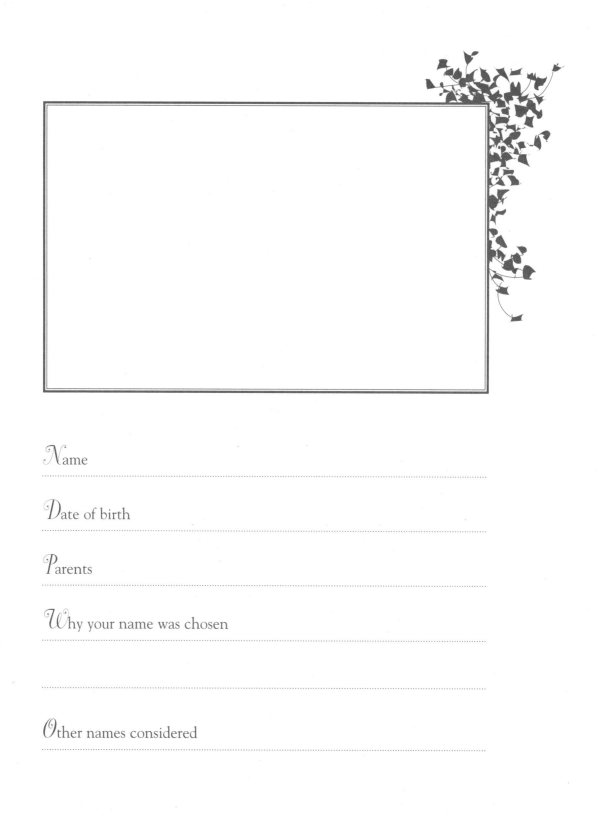

$\mathcal{N}$ame

....

$\mathcal{D}$ate of birth

....

$\mathcal{P}$arents

....

$\mathcal{W}$hy your name was chosen

....

....

$\mathcal{O}$ther names considered

....

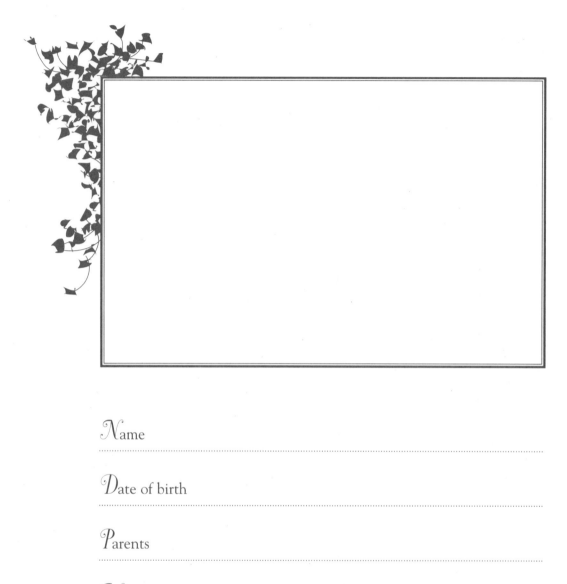

$\mathcal{N}$ame

....

$\mathcal{D}$ate of birth

....

$\mathcal{P}$arents

....

$\mathcal{W}$hy your name was chosen

....

....

$\mathcal{O}$ther names considered

....

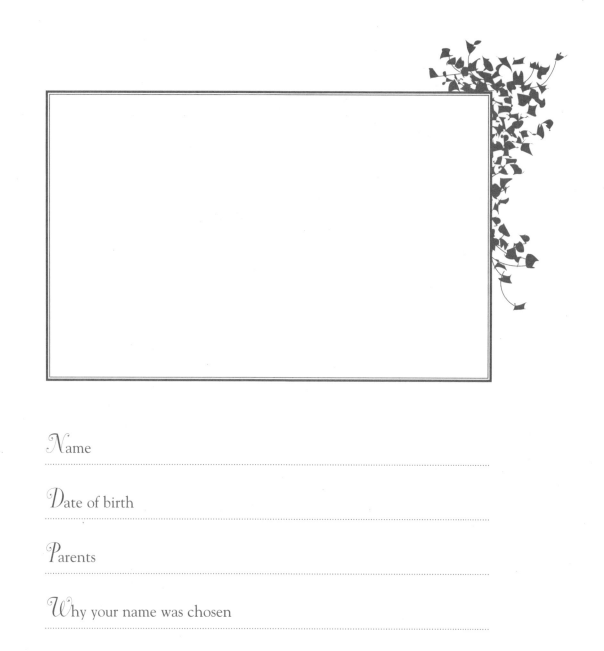

$\mathcal{N}$ame
....

$\mathcal{D}$ate of birth
....

$\mathcal{P}$arents
....

$\mathcal{W}$hy your name was chosen
....

....

$\mathcal{O}$ther names considered
....

Names

Girls' Names

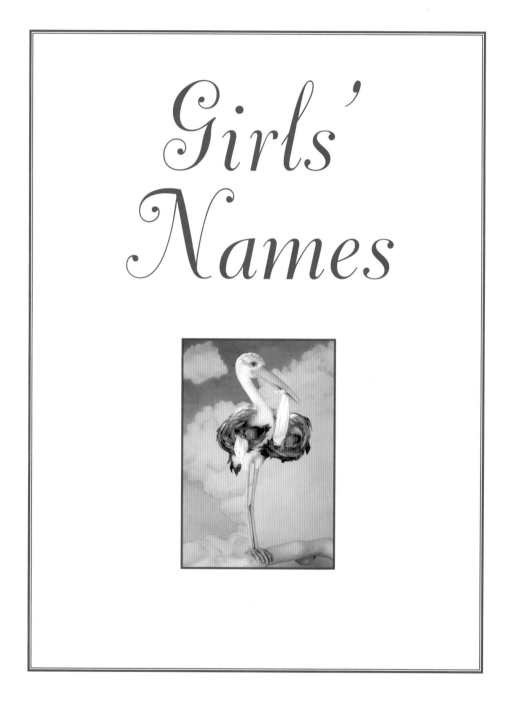

Abby, Abbie, Abbey, affectionate short forms of Abigail.

Abigail, "father rejoices," Hebrew.

Abra, feminine form of Abraham, "father of many," Hebrew.

Acton, originally a surname and boy's name meaning "from the town near the oaks," Old English.

Ada, "joyful," Hebrew.

Adah, "adornment, ornament," from the Old Testament, or an African name meaning "first born."

Adanna, "father's daughter," African.

Adda, variation of Ada.

Adela, variation of Adelaide.

Adelaide, "noble," Old German. Also a place name, a city in Australia.

Adele, French variation of Adelaide.

Adeline, French diminutive of Adele.

Adina, "voluptuous," Hebrew.

Adria, variation of Adriana.

Adrian, "from Hadria," Latin. Originally a boy's name.

Adriana, feminine form of Adrian.

Adrianne, variation of Adriana.

Adrienne, French form of Adriana.

Africa, "pleasant," Old Celtic. Used as a personal name after the continent.

Agatha, "good," Greek. The patron saint of firefighters.

Agave, "illustrious," Greek.

Agnes, "pure and holy," Greek. First borne by a young virgin martyr in the third century.

Aida, "she is arriving," borne by an Egyptian princess. The title of a Verdi opera.

Aidan, "little fire," Irish Gaelic. Originally a boy's name.

Aileen, Scottish form of Helen.

Ailsa, after the Scottish place name, Ailsa Craig.

Aimee, "beloved," French.

Aine, "brightness," Irish Gaelic.

Ainsley, Ainslee, Scottish surname meaning "meadow."

Aisha, from an African word meaning "life." The prophet Mohammed's favorite wife.

Aisleen, Aisling, Irish personal name meaning "dream" or "vision."

Alain, variation of Alaina.

Alaina, of uncertain origin, possibly Arabic, meaning "noble."

Alana, Alannah, Alanna, feminine forms of Alan, from the Celtic words for "spirit" and "rock."

Alberta, feminine form of Albert, derived from the Old German words for "noble" and "bright."

Albina, "white," Latin.

Alessandra, Italian form of Alexandra.

Alethea, "truth," Greek.

Alex, short form of Alexandra.

Alexa, variation of Alexandra.

Alexandra, feminine form of Alexander, "defender of men," Greek. A name with a royal pedigree of Roman, Russian and English queens.

Alexandria, variation of Alexandra.

Alexia, variation of Alexandra.

Alexis, originally a boy's name. A variation of Alexander, "defender of men," Greek.

Ali, short form of Alice or Alison.

Alice, from Old German, "nobility." The heroine of *Alice's Adventures in Wonderland*.

Alicia, Spanish form of Alice.

Alina, variation of Aline.

Aline, short form of Adeline, dating from the Middle Ages.

Alisa, variation of Alice.

Alison, originally a diminutive of Alice, from Old German, "nobility."

Alithea, variation of Alethea.

Allegra, from Italian, "lively." The familiar musical term "allegro" influenced its use as a first name.

Allie, short form of Alice or Alison.

Allison, variation of Alison.

Ally, short form of Alice or Alison.

Alma, "nourishing, kind," Latin. Popular as a name after the Battle of Alma in the Crimean War.

Almira, "from the city of Almira," Spanish.

Althea, with origins in Greek mythology, meaning "to heal."

Alyce, variation of Alice.

Alycia, variation of Alicia.

Alys, variation of Alice.

Alyssa, variation of Alicia.

Ama, "born on Saturday," African.

Amabel, "lovable," Latin.

Amanda, created in the 17th century for a play. From Latin, "lovable."

Amaryllis, "to sparkle," Greek.

Amber, "light," Egyptian. First used as a personal name in the 19th century, after the gem.

Amelia, from German, "work." Popularized in modern times by aviatrix Amelia Earhart.

Ameline, variation of Amelia.

Amina, Aminah, "peaceful, safe," African/Arabic. The mother of the prophet Mohammed.

Amy, English form of Aimee.

Ana, Spanish form of Anne.

Anabel, variation of Annabel.

Anais, from Hebrew, "graceful." Associated with Anais Nin, the Paris-born American novelist.

Anastasia, "resurrection," from Greek. The youngest daughter of the last Russian Tsar.

Anatolia, "from the east," from Greek.

Andrea, feminine form of Andrew, "warrior," Greek.

Angel, variation of Angela.

Angela, "messenger," Latin.

Angelica, "angelic," Latin.

Angelina, diminutive of Angela.

Anika, "sweet-faced," African. Also a Scandinavian diminutive of Anne.

Anita, Spanish diminutive of Ana.

Ann, variation of Anne.

Anna, variation of Anne.

Annabel, Annabelle, variations of Amabel, "lovable," Latin.

Anne, "God has favored," Hebrew. St. Anne was believed to be the name of the mother of the Virgin Mary and the name was popularized by her followers.

Annemarie, combination of Anne and Marie.

Annette, French diminutive of Anne.

Annice, variation of Annis.

Annie, diminutive of Anne.

Annis, medieval Scottish variation of Agnes.

Anthea, "flowery," Greek. A title of the mythological Greek goddess Hera revived by 17th-century poets.

Antoinette, French feminine form of Anthony, "worthy of praise," from Latin. Associated with Marie Antoinette, who was guillotined in the French Revolution.

Antonia, feminine form of Anthony.

Antonina, variation of Antonia.

Anwen, "beautiful," from Welsh.

Anya, variation of Anne.

April, "to open," Latin. From the name of the month.

Arabella, popular Scottish name from the Middle Ages. From Latin, "entreated."

Araminta, coined in 18th-century Britain.

Areta, variation of Aretha.

Aretha, from Greek, "virtue."

Ariadne, "very holy," Greek. In Greek mythology, the daughter of King Minos of Crete.

Arianna, variation of Ariadne.

Arianne, French form of Ariadne.

Ariel, "lion of God," Hebrew. Originally a boy's name.

Ariela, feminine variation of Ariel.

Arielle, feminine variation of Ariel.

Arlene, variation of Arline.

Arlette, "pledge," Norman French.

Arline, coined for the heroine of the 19th-century opera *The Bohemian Girl.*

Aroha, "love," New Zealand Maori.

Asha, "to hope, wish," Sanskrit. Also a variation of Aisha.

Ashanti, from an African tribe and place name.

Ashley, Ashleigh, "ash wood," Old English. Originally a place name and surname.

Asia, evocative of the continent, from Greek, "east."

Astra, "star," Greek.

Astrid, "fair, beautiful," Scandinavian.

Atalanta, "might bearer," in Greek mythology, a legendary huntress.

Athena, variation of Athene.

Athene, the goddess of wisdom in Greek mythology.

Atlanta, from the place name, the city in Georgia, U.S.A.

Aubrey, from German, "elf power." Historically a boy's name, but recently popular for girls.

Audrey, "noble and strong," Old English.

Augusta, feminine form of Augustus, "magnificent," Latin. The title of the female relatives of Roman emperors.

Aurelia, "golden," Latin.

Aurelie, French form of Aurelia.

Aurora, "dawn," Latin.

Autumn, the fall season, Latin.

Ava, from Old German, "bird."

Averil, variation of Avril, or from the Old English words for "boar" and "battle."

Avery, from the surname, a variation of Alfred.

Aviva, "spring," Hebrew.

Avril, French form of April.

Aysha, variation of Aisha.

Azalea, recently used as a name from the flowering shrub.

Azaria, originally a male biblical name, "helped by God," Hebrew.

Aziza, with Hebrew, African, and Arabic origins, meaning "victorious."

Babette, affectionate short form of Barbara or Elizabeth.

Bailey, surname from the Middle Ages denoting a "bailiff," Old English.

Baraka, "blessing," African.

Barbara, Barbra, "foreign woman," Latin. A name borne by an early Christian saint, the patron of architects and stonemasons.

Bathsheba, "daughter of the oath," Hebrew. In biblical times, the mother of Solomon.

Beatrice, "blessed voyages," Latin, or "one who brings joy." In literature, Beatrice was Dante's guide through Paradise and the heroine of Shakespeare's *Much Ado About Nothing.*

Beatrix, variation of Beatrice.

Beattie, Beatty, diminutives of Beatrice or Beatrix.

Becca, short form of Rebecca.

Becky, diminutive of Rebecca.

Bedelia, Irish affectionate form of Bridget.

Belinda, possibly from Italian, "beautiful."

Bella, "beautiful," Italian, or a short form of Isabella.

Belle, "beautiful," French.

Berenice, "bringer of victory," Greek.

Bernadette, "bold as a bear," French. Popular since a French girl of the same name had a vision of the Virgin Mary at Lourdes.

Bernice, variation of Berenice.

Bertha, Berthe, "bright," Old German.

Beryl, "pure," Greek, used as a name after the precious stone.

Bess, diminutive of Elizabeth.

Bessie, diminutive of Elizabeth.

Beth, affectionate short form of Elizabeth.

Bethany, "house of figs," Hebrew. A village near Jerusalem mentioned in the New Testament.

Betsy, affectionate short form of Elizabeth.

Bette, variation of Betty.

Bettina, variation of Betty.

Betty, affectionate short form of Elizabeth.

Beulah, biblical name for Israel meaning "married" in Hebrew.

Beverley, Beverly, originally a surname, from Old English, "beaver stream." Now from a place name, Beverly Hills.

Bianca, "white" or "pure," the Italian form of Blanche.

Biddie, Biddy, affectionate short forms of Bridget.

Bijou, "jewel," French.

Billie, feminine form of Billy, a diminutive of William.

Blair, Celtic family name meaning "plains."

Blaise, "lisping," from Latin. Originally a French name for a boy.

Blanche, "white," French. Originally a nickname for a blonde. The leading character in *A Streetcar Named Desire* by Tennessee Williams.

Blodwen, "white flower," Welsh.

Blossom, recently used as a name, from the word for flowers on a fruit tree, Old English.

Blythe, Blyth, "happy, carefree," Old English.

Bobbie, feminine form of Bobby, or a diminutive of Barbara or Roberta.

Bonita, "pretty," from Spanish.

Bonnie, "pretty," Scottish.

Brandy, Brandi, "burnt wine," Dutch, or a feminine form of Brandon, "prince," Celtic.

Bree, modern coinage.

Brenda, from Old Norse, "sword."

Brenna, recently coined as a name, a variation of Brianna.

Brett, originally a boy's name, an ethnic name for a Breton or Briton.

Brianna, Briana, feminine forms of Brian, "high," "noble," Celtic.

Briar, after the "wild, thorny rose bush," Old English.

Bridget, English form of an Irish Gaelic name meaning "strong." A patron saint of Ireland and a Celtic goddess of poetry and prophecy.

Bridgette, variation of Bridget.

Bridie, diminutive of the Irish form of Bridget.

Brigitte, French and German form of Bridget.

Briony, variation of Bryony.

Britany, variation of Brittany.

Britt, Swedish form of Bridget.

Brittany, "from Bretagne," referring to the region of France.

Brittney, Britney, variations of Brittany.

Bronwen, Bronwyn, Welsh personal name from the words for "breast" and "fair," or "blessed."

Brooke, Brook, originally a surname, "stream," Old English.

Bryn, Welsh name meaning "hill."

Bryna, variation of Brianna.

Brynm, variation of Bryn.

Bryony, "twining vine," Greek.

Caitlin, Irish Gaelic form of Catherine.

Caitlyn, Caitlynn, modern blends of Caitlin and Lynn.

Caitrin, Irish Gaelic form of Catherine.

Calista, variation of Callista.

Calla, variation of Callista.

Callie, variation of Callista.

Calliope, from Greek, the muse of poetry.

Callista, "most beautiful," Greek.

Callula, "small beautiful one," Latin.

Calypso, "silent one." In Greek literature, the sea nymph who captured Odysseus.

Camellia, from the name of the flowering shrub, Latin.

Camilla, "ceremonial attendant," Latin. The name of a warrior queen in Virgil's poetry.

Camille, French form of Camilla.

Canace, variation of Candace.

Candace, "fire white," Greek. Originally the title of a line of queens in ancient Ethiopia.

Candice, variation of Candace.

Candida, "white," Latin.

Candy, diminutive of Candace or Candida.

Caprice, Italian name meaning "fanciful."

Cara, recent coinage, from Italian, "beloved." Also from Irish Gaelic, "friend."

Carina, variation of Cara.

Carine, variation of Cara.

Carissa, "grace," Greek, or "dear one," Italian.

Carla, feminine form of Carl, "freeman," Old German.

Carlene, Carline, variations of Carla.

Carlotta, Italian form of Charlotte.

Carly, variation of Carla.

Carmel, "garden," from Hebrew. Also a title of the Virgin Mary.

Carmelina, variation of Carmel.

Carmelita, Spanish diminutive of Carmel.

Carmen, Spanish form of Carmel, also meaning "song," Latin.

Carmia, variation of Carmen.

Carmine, variation of Carmen.

Carmita, variation of Carmen.

Caro, short form of Caroline.

Carol, Carole, feminine forms of Charles, "freeman," Old German. Also from Gaelic, "melody, song."

Carolina, Italian and Spanish form of Caroline.

Caroline, feminine form of Charles, "freeman," Old German.

Carolyn, variation of Caroline.

Carrie, Carry, short forms of Caroline.

Carryl, variation of Carol.

Carson, originally a surname referring to the "son of a marsh-dweller," Old English.

Carter, originally a surname referring to a "cart-driver," Old English.

Casey, "vigilant," Irish Gaelic. Also a variation of Cassie.

Cass, short form of Cassandra.

Cassandra, in Greek mythology, a Trojan princess who had the gift of prophecy but was fated not to be believed after spurning Apollo.

Cassidy, originally an Irish Gaelic surname. Also a variation of Cassie.

Cassie, diminutive of Cassandra.

Catalina, Spanish form of Catherine.

Caterina, Italian form of Catherine.

Catharine, Catharyn, variations of Catherine.

Catherine, "pure," Old French, from Greek. Borne by saints and royals in France and Russia, notably by Catherine the Great of Russia.

Catheryn, variation of Catherine.

Cathie, diminutive of Catherine.

Cathleen, variation of Kathleen.

Cathryn, variation of Catherine.

Cathy, diminutive of Catherine.

Catlin, variation of Caitlin.

Catrin, Welsh form of Catherine.

Catrina, variation of Catriona.

Catriona, Scottish and Irish forms of Catherine.

Cecile, French form of Cecilia.

Cecilia, originally a Roman family name meaning "blind." The patron saint of music, after a third-century martyr.

Cecily, variation of Cecilia.

Celena, variation of Celine.

Celeste, "heavenly," a French personal name derived from Latin.

Celia, originally a Roman family name, from Latin, "heaven." Introduced to Britain by Shakespeare in the play *As You Like It*.

Celine, "heaven," French, from Latin.

Cerise, "cherry," French.

Chanel, originally a French surname meaning "canal," brought into use as a personal name in celebration of designer Coco Chanel.

Chanelle, variation of Chanel.

Chantal, French personal name meaning "singer."

Chantelle, variation of Chantal.

Charis, "grace," Greek. One of the Three Graces in Greek mythology.

Charissa, a modern blend of Charis and Carissa.

Charity, one of the three theological virtues, "faith, hope and charity," of Christian love. From Latin, "dear."

Charlene, Charleen, modern coinage based on Charles, "freeman," Old German.

Charlie, Charli, diminutives of Charlotte or Charlene.

Charlotta, Scandinavian form of Charlotte.

Charlotte, French feminine form of Charles, "freeman," Old German. Popularized by Queen Charlotte in the 17th century, and later by novelist Charlotte Bronte.

Charmaine, Charmain, modern variations of Charmian.

Charmian, from Greek, "delight."

Chastity, from Latin, "pure."

Chelsea, originally a place name in England meaning "landing place for chalk." Used in modern times as a personal name.

Chelsey, variation of Chelsea.

Cher, short form of Cherie or Cherilyn.

Cherie, French term of endearment, "dear, darling."

Cherilyn, possibly a blend of Cheryl and Carolyn.

Cherry, introduced by Charles Dickens as a diminutive of Charity.

Cheryl, modern coinage based on Cherry and possibly Beryl.

Cheyenne, from the name of the Native American tribe.

Chiara, Italian form of Clara.

China, used as a personal name after the name of the country.

Chloe, "new growth," the Greek goddess of fertility.

Chloris, from Greek, "green," a goddess of vegetation.

Chris, short form of names such as Christine.

Christa, variation of Christiana.

Christabel, from Latin, "Christ" and "beautiful."

Christiana, feminine form of Christian, "follower of Christ," Latin, originating in the Middle Ages.

Christie, diminutive of names such as Christine.

Christina, variation of Christiana.

Christine, "follower of Christ," French.

Christmas, from the festival celebrating Christ's birth.

Christy, variation of Christie.

Cicelle, variation of Cecilia.

Cicely, variation of Cecilia.

Cilla, short form of Priscilla.

Cinderella, from French, "little cinders."

Cindy, diminutive of Cynthia or Lucinda.

Claire, Clair, French forms of Clara.

Clara, from Latin, "clear" or "bright." In use since the Middle Ages.

Clare, variation of Clara.

Clarice, medieval French variation of Clara.

Clarinda, coined in Spenser's *The Faerie Queene*.

Clariss, variation of Clarice.

Clarissa, Latinized form of Clarice.

Claudette, French feminine form of Claudius, from Latin, "lame."

Claudia, Latin feminine form of Claudius.

Claudine, variation of Claudette.

Clea, short form of Cleantha.

Cleantha, "glory flower," Greek.

Clematis, "climbing plant," Greek.

Clementine, feminine form of Clement, "mild, gentle," Latin.

Cleo, short form of Cleopatra.

Cleopatra, "fame of her father," Greek. A name associated with the Queen of Egypt, the lover of Julius Caesar.

Clio, "glory," name of the Greek muse of history.

Clotilda, Clothilda, Clothilde, "famous battle maiden," Old German.

Clover, from the name of the plant.

Coleen, Colene, variations of Colleen.

Colette, from the medieval name Col, the short form of Nicholas.

Colleen, from the Irish Gaelic word for "girl."

Collette, variation of Colette.

Colombe, French form of Columba.

Columba, "dove," Latin.

Conception, "beginning," Latin.

Connie, short form of Constance.

Connor, English form of an Irish Gaelic name meaning "lover of hounds." Recently used as a first name for girls.

Constance, "constancy," Latin.

Constanta, variation of Constance.

Constantia, variation of Constance.

Consuela, feminine form of Consuelo, "consolation," Spanish.

Cora, from Greek, "maiden."

Coral, from the vocabulary word "coral."

Coralie, modern blend of Coral and Rosalie.

Cordelia, from "cor," Latin for "heart." The youngest, virtuous daughter of King Lear in Shakespeare's play of the same name.

Coretta, variation of Cora.

Corey, Cori, "from the hollow," Irish Gaelic.

Corina, variation of Corinna.

Corine, variation of Corinna.

Corinna, from Greek, "girl."

Corinne, variation of Corinna.

Cornelia, from the Latin feminine form of Cornelius, a Roman family name meaning "horn."

Cory, variation of Corey.

Cosette, "pet lamb," Teutonic.

Courteney, Courtenay, Courtney, originally a surname referring to a place in France.

Cressida, a Trojan princess in ancient legends. Possibly from Greek, "gold."

Cris, Criss, short forms of names such as Christine.

Crissy, diminutive of names such as Christine.

Crystal, a jewel name.

Cybil, variation of Sibyl.

Cynthia, a name for Artemis, the moon goddess, Greek, derived from the name of the island of her birth.

Dagmar, from the Old Scandinavian words for "day" and "maid."

Dahlia, from the name of the flower.

Daisy, from the name of the flower. A Victorian pet form of Margaret.

Dakota, from the name of the Native American nation and the place name.

Dale, originally a surname referring to someone from a "valley."

Dalia, variation of Dahlia. Also from Hebrew, "flowering branch."

Dallas, possibly from Gaelic, "wise." Also a place name.

Damaris, from the New Testament, possibly Greek, "calf."

Dana, "pure as day," Latin. Borne by a Celtic goddess of fertility.

Danae, "who judges," Greek.

Dania, Latin form of Denmark.

Daniela, Daniella, variations of Danielle.

Danielle, French feminine form of Daniel, "God is my judge," Hebrew.

Dannie, Danni, short forms of Danielle.

Danya, variation of Dania.

Daphne, from Greek mythology, a nymph who changed into a laurel bush to escape Apollo. The name of a flower.

Dara, feminine form of Darius, an ancient Persian personal name meaning "possessing good."

Darci, Darcie, variations of Darcy.

Darcy, from the French place name Arcy.

Daria, feminine form of Darius, an ancient Persian personal name.

Darla, variation of Darlene.

Darlene, Darleen, Darline, "dearly beloved," English.

Darrel, variation of Daryl.

Daryl, Darryl, originally a surname referring to Airelle in France. First used as a personal name for boys.

Davida, feminine form of David, "beloved," Hebrew.

Davina, Scottish feminine form of David.

Davinia, variation of Davina.

Dawn, "daybreak," a translation of Aurora, the Greek goddess of dawn.

Dayle, variation of Dale.

Dayna, variation of Dana.

Deana, Deanna, modern coinages, variations of Diana.

Debbie, Debby, short forms of Deborah.

Deborah, Debora, "bee," Hebrew. An Old Testament name.

Debra, variation of Deborah.

Decima, "tenth," Latin. Roman goddess of childbirth.

Dee, affectionate form of Dorothy, used also as a first name.

Deirdre, Deidre, of uncertain origin, borne by a tragic heroine of Irish mythology, "Deirdre of the Sorrows."

Delia, associated with Artemis, the moon goddess, Delos being the island of her birth. Brought into use as a name by 17th-century romantic poets.

Delicia, "delight," from Greek. First used as a name in modern times.

Delilah, of uncertain origin, the name of Samson's mistress in the Old Testament.

Della, of uncertain origin, possibly from Delilah or Adela.

Delores, Deloris, variations of Dolores.

Delphine, from the Greek place name Delphi, the site of Apollo's oracle.

Delwyn, from Welsh, "pretty, fair" or "blessed."

Delyth, Welsh, a modern coinage meaning "pretty."

Demetria, after Demeter, in Greek mythology, the goddess of fertility and harvest.

Demi, "half," French, from Latin.

Dena, modern coinage, possibly based on Dean.

Denise, Denice, feminine forms of Dennis, associated with the Greek god of wine.

Desdemona, from Greek, "ill-starred," the wife of Shakespeare's Othello.

Desiree, from French, "desired," once given to a longed-for child.

Destiny, "fortune" or "fate." Used as a personal name in modern times.

Devon, originally a surname referring to the English county.

Diamond, from the name of the jewel.

Diana, the Roman name for the Greek goddess Artemis, huntress and goddess of the moon.

Diane, variation of Diana.

Dianna, variation of Diana.

Dianne, variation of Diana.

Dilys, "genuine," Welsh.

Dinah, Dina, "judged," from Hebrew. In the Old Testament, the daughter of Jacob and Leah.

Dionne, feminine form of Dion, "God," from Latin.

Dixie, possibly from Dixon, meaning "son of Richard." Also the affectionate name for the American South.

Dolly, affectionate short form of Dorothy or Dolores.

Dolores, a title of the Virgin Mary. From Spanish, "sorrow."

Dominique, French feminine form of Dominic, from Latin, "of the Lord."

Donna, Dona, from Italian, "lady."

Dora, short form of Dorothea, used as a first name since the mid-19th century.

Dorean, "daughter of Finn," Irish Gaelic.

Doreen, Dorene, variations of Dora.

Doria, variation of Dora.

Doris, from Greek, "Dorian woman." In Greek mythology, a sea nymph.

Dorothea, from Greek, "gift" and "god."

Dorothy, English form of Dorothea.

Dot, affectionate short form of Dorothy or Dorothea.

Dottie, Dotty, affectionate forms of Dorothy or Dorothea.

Drew, short form of Andrew, now popular as a personal name for girls.

Dru, short form of Drusilla.

Drusilla, from an Old Roman family name meaning "dewy-eyed."

Dulcie, "charming, sweet," Latin.

Dyan, Dyanne, variations of Diana.

Eartha, "of the earth," Old English.

Easter, "spring," Old English. From the name of the Christian festival.

Ebony, from Greek, after the hard, dark wood.

Eda, "prosperity", Old English.

Eddie, Eddy, affectionate short forms of names such as Edwina.

Eden, "delight," Hebrew. In the Old Testament, the Garden of Eden.

Edie, Scottish diminutive of Edith.

Edith, derived from the Old English words for "rich, happy" and "war."

Edna, "delight, desired," Hebrew.

Edwina, feminine form of Edwin, "rich friend," Old English.

Effie, affectionate short form of Euphemia.

Egypt, used as a first name after the country.

Eileen, Irish form of Helen.

Eithne, "kernel," Irish Gaelic.

Elaine, French form of Helen.

Eldora, "golden one," Spanish.

Eleanor, German form of Helen.

Electra, from Greek, "shining one."

Elena, Italian and Spanish form of Helen.

Eliane, French form of a Latin family name meaning "sun."

Elinor, variation of Eleanor.

Elisa, short form of Elizabeth.

Elisabeth, biblical variation of Elizabeth.

Elise, French variation of Elizabeth.

Elissa, short affectionate form of Elizabeth.

Eliza, short form of Elizabeth.

Elizabeth, "oath of God," Hebrew. In the Old Testament, the mother of John the Baptist. A name borne by English royalty.

Ella, from Old German, "all."

Ellen, variation of Helen found as early as the Middle Ages.

Ellie, affectionate short form of Ellen.

Elodie, from Latin, "all wealth," and a flower name.

Eloise, modern French form of Heloise and Louise, meaning "healthy" and "wide."

Elsa, German short form of Elizabeth, or from German "noble."

Elsie, Scottish short form of Elizabeth.

Elspeth, Scottish form of Elizabeth.

Elvira, Spanish name originating in the Middle Ages. From Old German, "elf counsel."

Elyse, variation of Elise.

Emanuela, feminine form of Emmanuel, "God is with us," Hebrew.

Emelia, variation of Emily.

Emeline, variation of Emmeline.

Emelyn, variation of Emmeline.

Emerald, from the name of the precious gem.

Emilie, French form of Emily.

Emily, feminine form of an Old Roman family name meaning "rival." Popularized by writers Emily Bronte and Emily Dickinson in the 19th century.

Emlyn, Welsh, possibly from the same origins as Emily. Originally a boy's name.

Emma, from an Old German name derived from words meaning "universal." Popularized as a first name by Emma of Normandy, the mother of Edward the Confessor in medieval England.

Emmeline, variation of Ameline, popularized in modern times by suffragette Emmeline Pankhurst.

Emogene, variation of Imogen.

Ena, English form of Eithne.

Enid, of uncertain origin, possibly from the Celtic words for "soul" or "life." Borne in King Arthur legends by a woman of nobility.

Erica, feminine form of Eric, "ever ruler," Old Norse. Also another name for "heather."

Erika, German and Scandinavian form of Erica.

Erin, from Eriu, an Irish goddess, and the ancient name of Ireland itself.

Erina, variation of Erin.

Erma, variation of Irma.

Erna, short form of Ernesta.

Ernesta, feminine form of Ernest, "serious battle," Old German.

Ernestina, feminine form of Ernest.

Ernestine, feminine form of Ernest.

Ertha, variation of Eartha.

Esme, "loved," Old French, from Latin.

Esmee, variation of Esme.

Esmeralda, from Spanish, "emerald." Invented as a first name by Victor Hugo for the novel *The Hunchback of Notre Dame*.

Estella, variation of Estelle.

Estelle, from French, "star."

Ester, variation of Esther.

Esther, Persian form of Hadassah.

Ethel, from an Old English name derived from the word "noble."

Ethelle, variation of Ethel.

Etta, affectionate short form of Henrietta.

Eudora, from the Greek words for "good" and "gift." As a name, a modern coinage.

Eugenia, feminine form of Eugene, "well born," Greek.

Eugenie, French form of Eugenia.

Eulalia, from Greek, "sweet-speaking."

Eulalie, French form of Eulalia.

Eunice, Greek, "good victory."

Euphemia, "good repute," Greek.

Eustacia, feminine form of Eustace, "fruitful," Greek.

Eva, variation of Eve.

Evadne, "good," a name originating in Greek mythology.

Evangeline, "good tidings," Latin.

Eve, from the Hebrew word for "life." In the Old Testament, the first woman.

Eveleen, Irish variation of Evelina.

Evelina, from an Old German name meaning "pleasant."

Eveline, variation of Evelina.

Evelyn, variation of Evelina. Originally a name for boys.

Evie, variation of Eve.

Evita, variation of Eva.

Evonne, variation of Yvonne.

Fabia, from an Old German family name meaning "bean-grower."

Fabiola, diminutive of Fabia.

Fae, variation of Fay.

Faith, one of the three theological virtues, "belief in God."

Fallon, originally an Irish surname meaning "leader."

Fanny, diminutive of Frances.

Fantine, French personal name popularized by the heroine of *Les Miserables* by Victor Hugo.

Farrah, possibly from Arabic, "joy, happiness."

Fatima, Fatimah, "creator," Arabic. The favorite daughter of Mohammed.

Fawn, from the word for a young deer, Latin.

Fay, Faye, from Old French, "fairy."

Felice, Italian form of Felix, "lucky," Latin. Occasionally used as a girl's name.

Felicia, feminine form of Felix dating from medieval times.

Felicity, "luck" or "good fortune," Old French.

Fenella, variation of Finola.

Feodora, Russian form of Theodora.

Fern, from the plant name. Used as a personal name in modern times.

Fidelia, feminine form of Fidel, "faithful," Spanish.

Fifi, French diminutive of Josephine.

Filomena, Italian form of Philomena.

Finella, variation of Finola.

Finola, from an Irish Gaelic name meaning "white shoulder."

Fiona, "white" or "fair," Gaelic. First used as a first name by a Scottish poet in the 18th century. Also Welsh, meaning "vine."

Fionna, variation of Fiona.

Fiora, Italian form of Flora.

Flavia, from an Old Roman family name meaning "yellow" or "golden-haired."

Fleur, "flower," French. A name dating from the Middle Ages.

Flo, short form of Florence, Flora or Fleur.

Flora, "flower," Latin. In Roman mythology, the goddess of spring.

Florence, originally a medieval boy's name. Popularized as a girl's name by Florence Nightingale and its association with the Italian city of her birth.

Florenz, variation of Florence.

Florenza, variation of Florence.

Florenze, variation of Florence.

Floretta, variation of Flora.

Florette, variation of Flora.

Floria, variation of Flora.

Florida, "blooming," Spanish. Also a place name.

Florinda, variation of Flora.

Flower, from the English vocabulary word.

Fortune, from Latin, "good luck."

Fran, short form of Frances.

Frances, "from France," Latin.

Francesca, Italian form of Frances.

Francie, diminutive of Frances.

Francine, French form of Frances.

Francoise, French form of Frances.

Frannie, Franny, diminutives of Frances.

Freda, diminutive of Winifred meaning "peace," Old German.

Frederica, Frederika, feminine forms of Frederick, from the Old German words for "peace" and "ruler."

Freya, "lady." In Norse mythology, the goddess of love.

Frieda, variation of Freda.

Gabby, diminutive of Gabrielle.

Gabe, diminutive of Gabrielle.

Gabriela, Gabriella, variations of Gabrielle.

Gabrielle, French feminine form of Gabriel, "man of God," Hebrew.

Gaby, French diminutive of Gabrielle.

Gae, variation of Gay, or short form of Gaenor.

Gaenor, variation of Guinevere.

Gaia, from Greek mythology, the earth goddess.

Gail, short form of Abigail.

Gala, Russian short form of Galina.

Gale, variation of Gail.

Galina, Russian form of Helen, or from Greek, "calm."

Garnet, from the name of the gemstone.

Gay, Gaye, "lively," from French.

Gayle, variation of Gail.

Gaynor, from medieval times, a form of Guinevere.

Gazelle, from Arabic, a small antelope.

Geena, variation of Gena or Gina.

Gemma, Italian affectionate name from medieval times meaning "gem."

Gena, diminutive of Eugenia.

Gene, short form of Eugenia or Eugenie, or a variation of Jean.

Geneva, from Latin, "gateway." Associated with the city in Switzerland.

Genevieve, from Old German, derived from the words for "people" and "woman." The patron saint of Paris.

Georgette, French feminine form of George, "farmer," Greek.

Georgia, variation of Georgina. Also a place name.

Georgiana, variation of Georgina.

Georgina, Latinate feminine form of George, "farmer," Greek.

Georgine, French variation of Georgina.

Geraldine, feminine form of Gerald, "spear" and "rule," Old German. First used as a personal name in the 16th century.

Germaine, feminine form of the French name Germain, "brother."

Gerry, affectionate short form of Geraldine.

Gertrude, from the Old German words for "spear" and "strength."

Ghislain, Ghislaine, variations of Gisela.

Gianna, Italian form of Jane.

Gigi, French affectionate short form of Georgine or Virginie.

Gilda, from Old German, "sacrifice."

Gill, short form of Gillian.

Gillian, medieval feminine form of Julian.

Gina, short form of Georgina.

Ginette, French diminutive of Genevieve.

Ginevra, variation of Genevieve.

Ginger, from Greek, a spice. Also a diminutive of Virginia.

Ginny, affectionate short form of Virginia.

Gisela, from German, "pledge."

Gisele, Giselle, French forms of Gisela.

Gladys, Welsh form of Claudia.

Glenda, modern Welsh name derived from the words for "clean, pure" and "good."

Glenn, Glen, originally a surname, "valley," Gaelic.

Glenys, modern Welsh name from the word for "pure."

Gloria, "glory," Latin.

Gloriana, Glorianna, variations of Gloria.

Glynis, variation of Glenys.

Golda, "gold," Yiddish.

Goldie, English form of Golda.

Grace, from Latin, meaning "God's favor."

Gracie, diminutive of Grace.

Grainne, Irish Gaelic name meaning "love."

Grania, Granya, variations of Grainne.

Greer, "watchful mother," Greek.

Greta, Swedish short form of Margaret.

Gretchen, German diminutive of Margaret.

Gretel, German diminutive of Margaret.

Griselda, from the Old German words for "gray" and "battle."

Guinevere, originally a Welsh name meaning "blessed" and "soft." The wife of King Arthur who fell in love with Sir Lancelot.

Gwen, Welsh short form of Gwendolyn.

Gwenda, Welsh short form of Gwendolyn.

Gwendolyn, Gwendolen, derived from the Welsh words for "white" or "blessed" and "ring" or "bow."

Gwyn, variation of Gwen.

Gwyneth, after a Welsh place name.

Gwynne, variation of Gwen.

Gypsy, "bohemian" or "rover."

Hadassah, "myrtle," Hebrew.

Haidee, from Greek, "caressed" or "modest."

Hailey, variations of Hayley.

Halima, Mohammed's nurse, Arabic/African.

Halle, Hallie, diminutives of Harriet.

Hana, Hanna, variations of Hannah.

Hannah, from Hebrew, "favored with a child." In the Old Testament, the mother of Samuel the prophet.

Harmony, "agreement," Greek.

Harriet, feminine form of Henry, from Old German, "home" and "ruler."

Harriette, variation of Harriet.

Hattie, Hatty, diminutives of Harriet.

Hayley, Haylee, originally a surname meaning "hay clearing," Old English.

Hazel, from Old English, the word for the tree.

Heather, the name of a plant. First used as a personal name in the 19th century.

Hebe, "young," Greek. In Greek mythology, a goddess of youth.

Hedda, Scandinavian variation of Hedwig, "dispute," from Old German.

Heidi, German form of Adelaide.

Helen, "sun," Greek. In Greek legend, the wife of Menelaus, whose capture began the Trojan war.

Helena, variation of Helen.

Helene, French form of Helen.

Helga, "healthy, prosperous," Old Norse.

Heloise, French name of uncertain origin. Possibly a form of Louise.

Henrietta, feminine form of Henry, from Old German, "home" and "ruler."

Henriette, French feminine form of Henry.

Hephzibah, Hepzibah, from Hebrew, "delight in her."

Hera, "lady." In Greek mythology, a goddess and wife of Zeus.

Hermia, feminine form of Hermes, the messenger god of Greek mythology. Brought to use as a first name in Shakespeare's play *A Midsummer Night's Dream*.

Hermione, feminine form of Hermes. The daughter of Helen of Troy.

Hester, medieval English form of Esther.

Hetty, Hettie, affectionate short forms of Henrietta.

Hilary, "cheerful," Latin.

Hilda, Hilde, from German, "battle."

Hillary, variation of Hilary.

Hippolyta, first found in Greek mythology as the Queen of the Amazons.

Holly, Hollie, from the name of a tree associated with Christmas.

Honor, from Latin, "honorable."

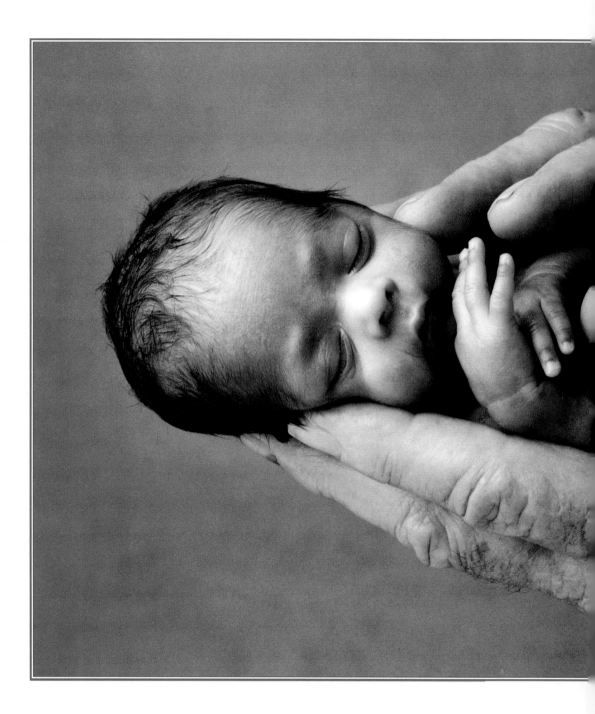

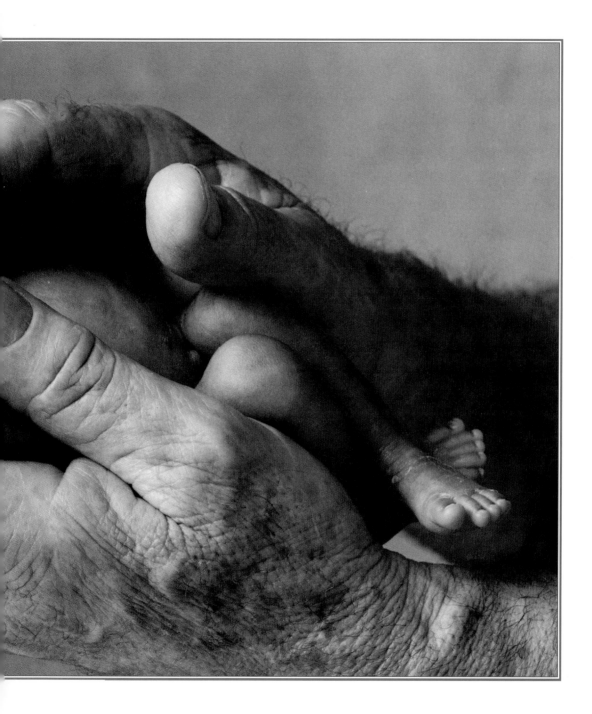

Honora, variation of Honor.

Honoria, variation of Honor.

Honour, variation of Honor.

Hope, one of the three theological virtues.

Horatia, feminine form of Horatius, an Old Roman family name meaning "keeper of the hours."

Hortense, French form of Hortensia.

Hortensia, from an Old Roman family name meaning "garden."

Hunter, from Old English, a surname for a "hunter."

Hyacinth, in Greek mythology, a youth killed accidentally by Apollo whose blood turned into the flower which bears his name. Now used for girls.

Hypatia, "highest," Greek.

Ianthe, "violet," Greek. In Greek mythology, the daughter of Oceanus, a god of the sea.

Ida, "work," Old German. Revived as the heroine of a Tennyson poem.

Idalia, in Greek mythology, one of the names of Aphrodite, the goddess of love.

Iesha, variation of Aisha.

Ilana, "tree," Hebrew.

Ileana, Romanian form of Helen.

Ilona, Hungarian form of Helen.

Ilsa, Ilse, German short forms of Elizabeth.

Iman, "faith," Arabic.

Imana, the name of an African god.

Imara, "firm," African.

Imelda, from the Old German words for "whole" and "battle."

Imogen, from a Celtic name meaning "innocent." First used by Shakespeare as the name for the heroine of his play *Cymbeline*.

Imogene, modern variation of Imogen.

Ina, short form of names such as Christina.

India, "river." Popularized as a girl's name by its association with the country.

Indira, "India," Hindi.

Indra, a god of early Hindu religion.

Ines, Inez, Spanish forms of Agnes.

Inga, Swedish short form of Ingrid.

Ingrid, Old Norse personal name meaning "fertility god" and "pretty."

Iola, "cloud at dawn," Greek.

Iolanthe, "violet," Greek.

Iole, original Greek form of Iola.

Iona, "island," Old Norse. An island in the Hebrides, a center of early Christianity.

Ione, a 19th-century coinage, possibly from the Greek word for "violet."

Irena, variation of Irene.

Irene, "peace," in Greek mythology, a goddess of peace.

Irina, Russian form of Irene.

Iris, "rainbow," Greek. In Greek mythology, the goddess of the rainbow and a messenger of the gods. Also the name of a flower.

Irma, "whole, universal," Old German.

Isa, diminutive of Isabel.

Isabel, Spanish form of Elizabeth.

Isabella, variation of Isabel.

Isabelle, variation of Isabel.

Isidora, Isadora, from Greek, "gift of Isis."

Isla, modern Scottish coinage, after the island of Islay.

Ismay, variation of Esme.

Isobel, Scottish form of Isabel.

Isolde, from Welsh, "beautiful." Name of a princess in King Arthur legends.

Ivie, variation of Ivy.

Ivory, recently popular as a first name through its association with Africa.

Ivy, from the word denoting the plant.

Izzie, Izzy, affectionate short forms of Isabel.

Jacinta, Spanish form of Hyacinth.

Jackie, Jacki, affectionate short forms of Jacqueline.

Jaclyn, variation of Jacqueline.

Jacqueline, feminine form of the French name Jacques, from Hebrew, "supplanter." Popularized by Jacqueline Kennedy Onassis.

Jacquelyn, variation of Jacqueline.

Jacquetta, variation of Jacqueline.

Jacqui, affectionate short form of Jacqueline.

Jade, from the name of the precious stone.

Jael, "wild goat," Hebrew. A biblical name.

Jaime, Spanish form of James, "supplanter," Hebrew. Now also used as a personal name for girls.

Jaimie, variation of Jaime.

Jaleesha, Jalisha, modern coinages blending "Ja-" with Lisa.

Jamaica, a place name.

Jamie, Jamee, feminine forms of James, "supplanter," Hebrew.

Jamila, "beautiful," African/Arabic.

Jan, short form of names such as Janet.

Jane, variation of Jehanne, from Hebrew, "Jehovah has favored."

Janelle, modern coinage derived from Jane.

Janet, diminutive of Jane from the Middle Ages that was revived in the late 19th century.

Janette, variation of Janet.

Janey, diminutive of Jane.

Janice, variation of Jane created for a novel in the 19th century.

Janie, diminutive of Jane.

Janine, variation of Jeannine.

Janis, variation of Janice.

Janna, modern coinage based on Jane.

Jannette, variation of Janet.

Jaquetta, variation of Jacqueline.

Jasmine, Jasmin, from the name of the flower, originally Persian.

Jay, Jaye, after the bird, or a short form of any "J" names.

Jayne, variation of Jane.

Jean, variation of Jehanne, from Hebrew, "Jehovah has favored," found mostly in Scotland.

Jeane, variation of Jean.

Jeanette, variation of Jean.

Jeanie, diminutive of Jean.

Jeanine, variation of Jeannine.

Jeanna, variation of Jean.

Jeanne, French feminine form of John.

Jeannette, variation of Jean.

Jeannie, diminutive of Jean.

Jeannine, French diminutive of Jeanne.

Jehanne, medieval French feminine form of John, "Jehovah has favored," Hebrew.

Jemima, "dove," from Hebrew. A biblical name.

Jemma, variation of Gemma, or a diminutive of Jemima.

Jen, short form of Jennifer.

Jenna, modern coinage based on Jennifer.

Jenni, Jennie, variations of Jenny.

Jennifer, Cornish form of Guinevere.

Jenny, affectionate form of Jane, Janet, Jean, or Jennifer, dating from the Middle Ages.

Jerri, Jerry, variations of Gerry.

Jess, short form of Jessica.

Jessamin, Jessamine, Jessamyn, variations of Jasmine.

Jesseca, variation of Jessica.

Jessica, possible biblical origins, meaning "God beholds," Hebrew. Popularized by Shakespeare in *The Merchant of Venice*.

Jessie, Jessy, Scottish affectionate forms of Janet, or short forms of Jessica.

Jewel, Jewell, from Old French, "gemstone."

Jezebel, "chaste," Hebrew. An Old Testament name.

Jill, short form of Jillian.

Jillian, variation of Gillian.

Jo, short form of Joanna, Joanne or Josephine.

Joan, from Old French Johanne, a feminine form of John, from Hebrew, "Jehovah has favored."

Joanna, variation of Joan.

Joanne, variation of Joan.

Jocasta, "shining moon," Greek.

Jocelyn, "merry," Latin.

Jody, Jodi, diminutives of Judith or Jo.

Johanna, Latinate form of Joan.

Jolanda, variation of Yolande.

Jolande, variation of Yolande.

Joni, Jonie, variations of Joan.

Jordan, "flowing down," Hebrew, after the biblical river.

Jordana, variation of Jordan.

Jordanne, variation of Jordan.

Josephine, feminine form of Joseph, meaning "may Jehovah add (another child)," Hebrew. One of the most famous bearers of this name was the wife of Napoleon Bonaparte.

Josette, French affectionate short form of Josephine.

Josie, affectionate short form of Josephine.

Joslyn, variation of Jocelyn.

Joss, short form of Jocelyn.

Joy, from Old French, "joyful in God." First used as a name in the Middle Ages.

Joyce, "merry," Latin. Originally a boy's name from the Middle Ages, revived as a girl's name in the 19th century.

Juanita, Spanish feminine diminutive of John, from Hebrew, "Jehovah has favored."

Judi, affectionate form of Judith.

Judith, from the Old Testament, "Jewess" or "from Judah," Hebrew.

Judy, affectionate form of Judith. Popularized as an independent name by actress Judy Garland.

Juli, variation of Julie.

Julia, feminine form of Julius, an Old Roman family name. Popularized by Shakespeare in *Two Gentlemen of Verona*.

Juliana, Julianna, feminine forms of Julian from the Middle Ages.

Julie, French form of Julia.

Juliet, Juliette, variations of Julia.

June, from the name of the month.

Juno, the wife of Jupiter in Roman mythology. Also an Irish variation of Una.

Justina, variation of Justine.

Justine, feminine form of Justin, "just, honest," Latin.

Kai, "ocean," Hawaiian, or from Welsh, "keeper of the keys."

Kailey, variation of Kayley.

Kaitlyn, variation of Caitlin.

Kali, "dark goddess," Sanskrit.

Kalila, "close friend," Arabic.

Kalindi, an Indian river, Hindi.

Kamilla, Kamila, variations of Camilla.

Kanisha, modern African-American coinage.

Kara, variation of Cara.

Karen, Danish form of Katherine.

Karin, Swedish form of Katherine.

Karina, from Latin, "keel."

Karissa, variation of Carissa.

Karla, feminine form of Karl, "freeman," Old German.

Karlee, Karlie, variation of Carla.

Karmel, variation of Carmel.

Karmela, variation of Carmel.

Karyn, Danish form of Katherine.

Kate, short form of Katherine.

Katelin, Katelyn, variations of Caitlin.

Katerina, Swedish form of Katherine.

Katharina, Russian form of Katherine.

Katharine, Katharyn, variations of Katherine.

Katherine, from Greek origins, meaning "pure." First brought to prominence in the third century by St. Katherine, who was executed for her Christian beliefs.

Katheryn, variation of Katherine.

Kathleen, variation of Caitlin, an Irish variation of Catherine, "pure," Greek.

Kathryn, variation of Katherine.

Kathy, affectionate short form of Katherine.

Katie, diminutive of Katherine.

Katrina, variation of Catriona.

Katrine, German form of Katherine.

Katy, diminutive of Katherine.

Katya, Russian affectionate form of Katherine.

Kay, Kaye, originally a short form of names beginning with "K."

Kayla, modern coinage based on Kay.

Kayley, Kaylee, modern coinages, possibly based on a surname.

Kaylyn, modern coinage blending Kay and Lyn.

Keisha, of uncertain origin, possibly African.

Kelly, Kellie, Kelley, from a traditional Irish Gaelic personal name, possibly meaning "church."

Kelsey, Kelsie, Kelsi, originally a surname, derived from Old English words for "ship" and "victory."

Kendall, originally a Celtic surname meaning "chief of the valley."

Kendra, modern coinage dating to the 1940s, possibly originating as a feminine form of Kendrick or Kenneth.

Kenya, "mountains of whiteness," the name of the east African country.

Keren, short form of the Old Testament name Kerenhappuch, "animal horn," Hebrew.

Keri, variation of Kerry.

Kerren, variation of Keren.

Kerrie, variation of Kerry.

Kerry, "descendants of Ciar," Irish Gaelic. The name of a county in Ireland.

Keshia, variation of Keisha.

Keziah, Kezia, from Hebrew, "cassia tree."

Kiara, variation of Clara.

Kim, short form of Kimberley.

Kimberley, Kimberly, originally a surname meaning "wood of Cyneburga." Also popular through its association with the South African city.

Kinsey, "royal victory," Old English.

Kiri, "bark of a tree," New Zealand Maori.

Kirsten, Scandinavian form of Christine.

Kirstie, variation of Kirsty.

Kirstin, variation of Kirsten.

Kirsty, originally a Scottish diminutive of Christiana.

Kit, affectionate form of Katherine.

Kitty, affectionate form of Katherine.

Klara, variation of Clara.

Korinna, original Greek form of Corinna.

Kris, diminutive of names such as Kristina.

Kristen, Kristin, variations of Christine from Scandinavia.

Kristie, variation of Christie.

Kristina, Scandinavian form of Christina.

Kristine, Scandinavian form of Christine.

Kristy, variation of Christie.

Krystle, variation of Crystal.

Kylie, of Australian origin, possibly relating to an Aboriginal word for "boomerang."

Lacey, originally a surname derived from the French place name Lassy.

Laetitia, variation of Letitia.

Laila, variation of Leila.

Lakeisha, modern coinage from adding "La-" to Keisha.

Lalage, "chatter," from Greek literature.

Lalia, "speech," Greek.

Lana, diminutive of Alana, or from Latin, "woolly," or a Russian diminutive of Svetlana.

Lane, originally a surname referring to someone who lived by a "lane or path."

Lani, "sky," Hawaiian.

Lanna, variation of Alanna.

Lara, Russian short form of Larissa. Popularized by the novel and film *Dr. Zhivago* and the musical piece from the film, "Lara's Theme."

Laraine, variation of Lorraine.

Larch, from the name of the tree, Latin.

Larissa, Russian personal name. From Latin, "laughing" and "cheerful."

Latasha, modern coinage blending "La-" and Tasha.

Latisha, modern form of Letitia.

Latoya, modern coinage popularized by Latoya Jackson.

Laura, from Latin, "bay tree." Originally a Latin boy's name, and immortalized in the love poetry of Italian poet Petrarch in the 14th century.

Laurel, Old French, from Latin, "bay tree."

Lauren, modern coinage, possibly a feminine form of Laurence.

Lauretta, Italian diminutive of Laura.

Laurette, French diminutive of Laura.

Laurie, Lauri, diminutives of Laura.

Lavender, from the name of the herb, Old French.

Laverne, originally a French surname meaning "alder grove."

Lavinia, from the Latin place name Lavinium. In Roman mythology, the wife of Aeneas and mother of the Roman people.

Layla, "wine," Arabic.

Lea, variation of Lee or Leah.

Leah, "languid," Hebrew. In the Old Testament, the elder sister of Rachel and wife of Jacob.

Leandra, feminine form of Leander, from Greek, "lion" and "man."

Leanne, modern blend of Lee and Anne, or a variation of Liane.

Leda, from Greek mythology, the Queen of Sparta.

Lee, originally a surname meaning "from the wood," Old English.

Leesa, Leeza, variations of Lisa.

Leia, variation of Lea. Popularized by Princess Leia in the *Star Wars* trilogy.

Leigh, variation of Lee.

Leila, "dark night," Arabic. Made popular in the 19th century by Byron's poetry.

Leilani, "garlanded," Hawaiian.

Lena, short form of names ending: "-lena."

Lenora, variation of Eleanor.

Lenore, variation of Eleanor.

Leona, feminine form of Leo or Leon, from Latin, "lion."

Leonie, French feminine form of Leon.

Leonora, variation of Eleanor.

Leonore, variation of Eleanor.

Lesley, Leslie, originally a Scottish surname, possibly from Gaelic, "court of hollies." Lesley is the usual feminine spelling.

Leta, "glad," Latin.

Leticia, variation of Letitia.

Letitia, "gladness," from Latin.

Lettice, in medieval times, the most popular form of Letitia.

Letty, affectionate short form of Letitia.

Lexie, affectionate short form of Alexandra.

Lia, variation of Leah.

Liana, diminutive of Juliana, or from French, "climbing vine."

Liane, short form of Eliane.

Lianne, variation of Leanne or Liane.

Libby, Libbie, affectionate short forms of Elizabeth.

Lila, variation of Leila.

Lilac, from the name of the flowering shrub.

Lili, German diminutive of Elizabeth, or chosen because of its association with the flower.

Lilian, from Latin, "lily," or a diminutive of Elizabeth.

Lilith, "night monster," Hebrew. In medieval folklore, the wife of Adam before Eve who was turned into a demon.

Lilla, Lillah, variations of Lilian, or diminutives of Elizabeth.

Lillian, variation of Lilian.

Lily, from the name of the flower, a symbol of purity.

Lina, diminutive of names ending "-lina," or a variation of Lena.

Linda, from Old German, "serpent," or from Spanish, "pretty."

Lindsay, Lindsey, originally a Scottish surname derived from a place name.

Lindy, variation of Linda.

Linnette, variation of Lynette.

Lisa, originally a diminutive of Elizabeth.

Lisabeth, variation of Elizabeth.

Lisbeth, variation of Elizabeth.

Lise, German diminutive of Elizabeth.

Lisette, French diminutive form of Elizabeth.

Livia, from Roman times, a variation of Olivia.

Liz, diminutive of Elizabeth.

Liza, diminutive of Elizabeth.

Lizzie, Lizzy, diminutives of Elizabeth.

Lois, from Greek, "good, desirable."

Lola, Spanish diminutive of Dolores.

Lolita, Spanish diminutive of Dolores. Associated with Vladimir Nabokov's infamous young heroine of the novel by the same name.

Lonny, from German. "Kind, excellent cook."

Lora, German form of Laura.

Loralie, variation of Lorelei.

Lorelei, "siren of the river," Teutonic.

Lorelie, variation of Lorelei.

Lorelle, variation of Lora.

Loren, variation of Lauren.

Loretta, variation of Lauretta. Also associated with Loreto in Italy, a place of Catholic pilgrimage.

Lorna, invented by author R.D. Blackmore for his novel *Lorna Doone*.

Lorraine, originally a surname referring to someone from the French region.

Lorrie, affectionate short form of Lorraine, or a variation of Laurie.

Lotte, German short form of Charlotte.

Lottie, originally an affectionate short form of Charlotte.

Louisa, variation of Louise.

Louise, French feminine form of Louis, from Old German, "famous warrior."

Luce, variation of Lucia.

Lucetta, diminutive of Lucia.

Lucette, diminutive of Lucia.

Lucia, feminine form of Lucius, an Old Roman personal name meaning "light."

Lucilla, diminutive of Lucia.

Lucille, French variation of Lucia.

Lucina, variation of Lucia.

Lucinda, variation of Lucia found in Cervantes' *Don Quixote*.

Lucretia, from an Old Roman family name meaning "gain." In Roman legend, the name of the maiden who killed herself after being raped by the King of Rome.

Lucy, variation of Lucia dating to the Middle Ages.

Luisa, variation of Louise.

Luise, German form of Louise.

Lulu, diminutive of Louise.

Luna, "moon," Latin.

Lydia, "woman of Lydia," Greek.

Lyn, variation of Lynn, or short form of Lynette.

Lynda, variation of Linda.

Lynette, Old French, originating from a Welsh name found in Arthurian legends. Also a diminutive of Lynn.

Lynn, "stream," Old English.

Lynnette, variation of Lynette.

Lynsey, variation of Lindsay.

Lyssa, short form of Alyssa.

Mab, "mirthful joy," Gaelic.

Mabel, variation of Amabel dating from the 12th century.

Mabelle, variation of Mabel.

Mackenzie, originally from a Scottish surname and a boy's name meaning "comely."

Mada, variation of Madeline.

Maddy, variation of Madeline.

Madeleine, French form of Madeline.

Madeline, derived from the personal name Magdalene, meaning "woman of Magdala." Introduced to Britain in the Middle Ages.

Madelyn, variation of Madeline.

Madge, diminutive of Margaret.

Madison, originally a surname meaning "son of Maud," Middle English. One of the few surnames to be derived from a woman's name.

Madonna, "My Lady," Italian. The title of the Virgin Madonna.

Mae, variation of May.

Maeve, from an ancient Irish name meaning "intoxicating." Borne by the Queen of Connaught in Irish legend.

Magda, German diminutive of Magdalene.

Magdalen, variation of Magdalene.

Magdalena, variation of Magdalene.

Magdalene, from the name of Mary Magdalene in the New Testament, Hebrew, meaning "woman from Magdala."

Maggie, diminutive of Margaret.

Magnolia, from the name of the flowering shrub or tree.

Mahalah, Mahala, "tenderness," Hebrew.

Mai, variation of May. Also a Swedish diminutive of Maria.

Maida, variation of Maidie.

Maidie, from "maid," originally meaning "girl," and first used as a nickname.

Maire, Irish Gaelic form of Mary.

Mairead, Irish Gaelic form of Margaret.

Maisie, Scottish diminutive of Margaret.

Mallory, originally a surname, derived from Old French, "unhappy, unlucky."

Malorie, Malory, variations of Mallory.

Malvina, invented as a personal name by Scottish poet James Macpherson.

Mamie, American diminutive of Mary.

Mandy, Mandie, Mandi, diminutives of Amanda.

Manon, French diminutive of Marie.

Mara, Marah, "bitter," Hebrew.

Marcella, feminine form of Marcellus, a Roman family name referring to Mars, the god of war.

Marcelle, French feminine form of Marcel, after Mars, the Roman god of war.

Marcia, feminine form of Marcius, a Roman family name derived from Mars.

Marcie, Marcy, variations of Marcia.

Marga, short form of Margaret.

Margaret, common medieval personal name derived from Greek, "pearl." First borne by martyred St. Margaret of Antioch in the fourth century.

Margery, variation of Marjorie.

Margot, affectionate short form of Marguerite.

Marguerita, variation of Margaret.

Marguerite, French form of Margaret.

Mari, Welsh form of Mary.

Maria, Latin, Italian, French and German form of Mary, "wished-for child," Hebrew.

Mariah, variation of Maria.

Mariamne, variation of Miriam, thought to be close to the original form of the name of the Virgin Mary.

Marian, medieval spelling of Marion, a diminutive of Mary.

Marianne, French diminutive of Marie.

Marie, French form of Mary, "wished-for child," Hebrew.

Mariel, short form of Mariella.

Mariella, Italian diminutive of Maria.

Marietta, Italian diminutive of Maria.

Mariette, French diminutive of Marie.

Marigold, from the name of the flower, its name derived from Old English "gold," the color, and "Mary," referring to the Virgin Mary.

Marilyn, modern blend of Mary and Lynn.

Marina, feminine form of the Latin family name Marinus, "of the sea."

Marion, medieval French diminutive of Mary.

Marisa, Marissa, variations of Maria.

Marjorie, Marjory, from Margerie, a French diminutive of Marguerite.

Marla, modern coinage based on Marlene.

Marlene, name coined for actress Marlene Dietrich, a contraction of her name, Maria Magdalene.

Marna, Swedish variation of Marina.

Marnie, Marny, variations of Marina.

Marquita, variation of Marcia.

Marsha, variation of Marcia.

Martha, from Aramaic, "lord." In the New Testament, the sister of Lazarus.

Marti, Martie, short forms of Martina.

Martina, feminine form of Martin, from Mars, the Roman god of war.

Martine, French form of Martina.

Marty, short form of Martina.

Mary, Middle English form of Miriam, Hebrew, probably meaning "wished-for child." The name of the Virgin Mary and Mary Magdalene.

Marya, Russian form of Mary.

Matilda, from a German personal name derived from the words for "might" and "battle."

Mattie, Matty, diminutives of Martha or Matilda.

Maud, Maude, variations of Matilda dating to the Middle Ages.

Maura, Celtic form of Mary.

Maureen, from an Irish Gaelic affectionate form of Maire.

Mavis, "song thrush," Old French.

Max, short form of Maximilian, a boy's name meaning "the greatest," Latin.

Maxine, French diminutive of Max, or a variation of Margaret or Mary.

May, from the name of the month, or a diminutive of Margaret or Mary.

Maya, variation of Roman goddess Maia, from Greek, "great," or from the name of the Indian tribe of Central and South America, or a variation of May.

Meagan, variation of Megan.

Meg, diminutive of Margaret.

Megan, Welsh affectionate form of Meg.

Mehitabel, Mehetabel, "favored of God," Hebrew.

Mel, short form of Melania or Melanie.

Melania, "black," Greek.

Melanie, French form of Melania.

Melinda, based on Melissa, coined by an 18th-century poet.

Melisande, medieval form of Millicent.

Melissa, from Greek, "honey bee."

Melody, Melodie, from Greek, "song."

Mercedes, "mercies," Spanish.

Mercia, from Old English, "people of the borderland."

Mercy, from the vocabulary word.

Meredith, Old Welsh, "great lord," originally a boy's name.

Meriel, variation of Muriel.

Merle, short form of Muriel. Also from Old French, "blackbird."

Merrily, from the word "merry."

Meryl, variation of Muriel.

Mia, Scandinavian diminutive of Maria.

Michael, "who is like Jehovah," Hebrew. Originally a boy's name.

Michaela, feminine form of Michael.

Michal, "brook," Hebrew. The wife of King David in the Old Testament.

Michele, Michelle, French feminine forms of Michael, "who is like Jehovah," Hebrew.

Mignon, from the French word for "darling."

Mikki, affectionate form of Michaela.

Mildred, from an Old English name derived from the words for "mild" and "strength."

Millicent, derived from the Old German words for "labor" and "strength."

Millie, Milly, diminutives of names such as Amelia, Camilla, Emily and Millicent.

Mimi, Italian affectionate form of Maria.

Mindy, variation of Mandy.

Minerva, "wisdom," Latin. The goddess of wisdom in Roman mythology.

Minna, from Old German, "love."

Minnie, originally a Scottish diminutive of Mary.

Mira, variation of Myra.

Mirabel, Mirabelle, "wonderful," from Latin.

Miranda, "admirable," Latin. Introduced by Shakespeare for the heroine of *The Tempest*.

Miriam, the original Hebrew form of Mary, probably meaning "wished-for child." In the Old Testament, the sister of Moses.

Mitzi, German diminutive of Maria.

Moana, "ocean," New Zealand Maori.

Modesty, from the vocabulary word.

Moira, English form of Maire, itself the Irish form of Mary.

Molly, Mollie, originally diminutives of Mary.

Mona, "noble," Irish Gaelic.

Monica, thought to be from either Greek, meaning "alone," or Latin, "to advise."

Monique, French form of Monica.

Morag, diminutive of Mor, "sun," Gaelic, a popular medieval Irish name.

Moreen, Irish affectionate form of Mor, "sun."

Morgan, from Old Welsh, "circle." Borne by King Arthur's sister, the sorceress.

Morgana, variation of Morgan.

Morna, "beloved," Gaelic.

Morwenna, "maiden," an ancient Celtic personal name.

Moya, modern coinage based on Mary.

Moyra, variation of Moira.

Muriel, from Irish Gaelic, "bright" and "sea." A Celtic personal name found in the Middle Ages.

Murphy, originally an Irish surname, "sea warrior."

Myra, coined for a 17th-century romantic poem.

Myrna, variation of Morna.

Myrtle, from the name of the flowering shrub, Latin.

Nada, variation of Nadia.

Nadia, from Russian, "hope."

Nadine, French variation of Nadia.

Nan, affectionate form of Anne or Nancy.

Nance, variation of Nancy.

Nancy, originally a variation of Anne.

Nanette, variation of Nan.

Nanni, Nanny, diminutives of Anne.

Naomi, "pleasantness," Hebrew.

Nat, short form of Natalia.

Natalia, Russian name, from Latin, "Christmas Day."

Natalie, French form of Natalia.

Natalya, variation of Natalia.

Natasha, Russian affectionate form of Natalia.

Neda, Nedda, "born on Sunday," Slavic.

Nell, affectionate short form of Eleanor, Ellen or Helen.

Nellie, Nelly, affectionate short forms of Eleanor, Ellen or Helen.

Nena, variation of Nina.

Nerida, "blossom," Australian Aboriginal.

Nerissa, from Shakespeare's play *The Merchant of Venice,* derived from Greek, "sea sprite."

Nerys, "lord," from Welsh, a modern coinage.

Nessa, traditional Irish Gaelic personal name. From Old Norse, "headland."

Nessie, Welsh diminutive of Agnes.

Nesta, Welsh diminutive of Agnes.

Neta, Netta, "shrub," or Scottish diminutive of Janet.

Nevada, from Spanish, "snowy." Also a place name.

Ngaio, New Zealand Maori, the name of a tree.

Nichola, variation of Nicola.

Nichole, variation of Nicola.

Nicholette, diminutive of Nicola.

Nicky, Nicki, affectionate forms of names such as Nicola.

Nicola, Italian feminine form of Nicholas, "victory" and "people," Greek.

Nicole, French form of Nicola.

Nicolette, French diminutive of Nicola.

Nikita, from Greek, "unconquerable." Originally a Russian boy's name.

Nikki, diminutive of names such as Nicola.

Nila, from the name of the Nile River, once borne by an Egyptian princess.

Nina, Russian short form of Antonina.

Ninette, French diminutive of Nina.

Niobe, "tearful," Greek.

Nita, diminutive of Juanita or Anita.

Nixie, "water sprite," German.

Noel, "Christmas," Old French.

Noeleen, Noeline, variations of Noel.

Noelle, variation of Noel.

Nola, possibly a diminutive of Finola or a feminine form of Nolan, meaning "chariot-fighter."

Nolene, modern Australian coinage, a feminine form of Nolan, or a variation of Noel.

Nona, "ninth," from Latin.

Noora, "camp," Australian Aboriginal.

Nora, Norah, Irish short forms of Honora.

Noreen, Irish diminutive of Nora.

Norma, "rule," Latin.

Nova, "new," Latin.

Oba, African river goddess.

Octavia, feminine form of Octavius, "eighth," Latin.

Odele, variation of Odile.

Odelia, "fatherland," Old German.

Odessa, from Greek, "long journey." The name of a Russian city.

Odette, French diminutive of Odile.

Odile, Odille, French forms of Odelia.

Ola, "descendant," Scandinavian.

Olga, Russian form of Helga.

Olive, from the name of the plant symbolizing peace.

Olivia, Italian form of Olive, first used as a personal name by Shakespeare in *Twelfth Night*.

Olwen, derived from the Welsh words for "footprint" and "white" or "fair."

Olympia, "from Olympus," Greek. Olympus was the home of the gods in Greek mythology.

Oona, Oonagh, variations of Una.

Opal, from the name of the gemstone.

Ophelia, from Greek, "help." The name of the tragic heroine in Shakespeare's *Hamlet*.

Ophrah, "fawn," Hebrew. The spelling Oprah has been popularized by television star Oprah Winfrey.

Oralia, variation of Aurelia.

Oralie, variation of Aurelie.

Oriana, "rise," Latin.

Oriel, from Old German, "fire" and "strife."

Orla, from the Irish Gaelic words for "gold" and "princess." First found in medieval times.

Orpah, "plucked," Hebrew. An Old Testament name.

Ottalie, Ottilie, feminine forms of Otto, "wealth, prosperity," Old German.

Page, Paige, "child," Greek.

Pallas, another name for Athene, the Greek goddess of wisdom.

Palma, Spanish place name, or from the name of a palm.

Paloma, "dove," Spanish.

Pam, short form of Pamela.

Pamela, possibly meaning "all honey," from Greek. Invented by poet Sir Philip Sidney and popularized by Samuel Richardson's novel *Pamela*.

Pandora, "all" and "gift," from Greek. In Greek mythology, the woman who released all the evils in the world.

Pansy, from the name of the flower.

Parker, "park-keeper," Old English. Originally a surname and then a boy's name.

Pat, short form of Patricia.

Patience, from Latin, a Christian virtue.

Patrice, Old French form of Patricia.

Patricia, feminine form of Patrick, from Latin, "nobleman."

Patsy, diminutive of Patricia.

Patty, Pattie, Patti, affectionate short forms of Patricia.

Paula, German feminine form of Paul, from Latin, "small."

Paulette, French diminutive of Pauline.

Paulina, variation of Paula.

Pauline, French form of Paulina.

Pearl, "sea mussel," from Old French.

Peg, affectionate form of Margaret.

Peggy, Peggie, affectionate forms of Margaret.

Penelope, "worker of cloth," Greek.

Penny, diminutive of Penelope.

Perdita, "lost," Latin. First used as a name by Shakespeare in *The Winter's Tale*.

Perpetua, "perpetual," Latin.

Persephone, "inspiring," Greek. In mythology, the daughter of Demeter who spent a third of the year in the underworld.

Persia, from the name of the ancient kingdom.

Persis, "woman from Persia," Greek.

Peta, modern coinage, a feminine form of Peter, "stone," Greek.

Petra, "stone," Greek.

Petrina, Russian form of Petra.

Petronella, Petronilla, feminine forms of the Roman family name Petronius, ultimately from Greek, "stone."

Petula, modern coinage, possibly from Latin, "to seek" or "to attack."

Phaedra, "bright one," Greek. In Greek mythology, the wife of Theseus.

Phaidra, variation of Phaedra.

Phebe, variation of Phoebe.

Phedra, variation of Phaedra.

Philadelphia, "brotherly love," Greek. A place name.

Philippa, Latinate feminine form of Philip, "lover of horses," Greek.

Philis, variation of Phyllis.

Phillida, variation of Phyllis.

Phillis, variation of Phyllis.

Philomena, "I am loved," Greek.

Phoebe, "bright one." In Greek mythology, the sister of Apollo.

Phylicia, variation of Felicia.

Phylida, Phyllida, variations of Phyllis.

Phyllis, "leafy." In Greek mythology, the daughter of the King of Thrace who killed herself for love and became the source of the almond tree.

Pia, "pious," Latin.

Pip, diminutive of Philippa.

Pippa, diminutive of Philippa.

Pixie, an elf.

Polly, affectionate form of Mary.

Pollyanna, from Polly and Anna, invented for the novel of the same name.

Poppy, from Old English, a flower.

Porsha, variation of Portia.

Portia, feminine form of the Roman family name Portius, "an offering." The heiress in Shakespeare's *The Merchant of Venice*.

Primrose, from the name of the flower, Latin.

Priscilla, feminine variation of the Roman family name Priscus, "ancient," Latin.

Pru, diminutive of Prudence or Prunella.

Prudence, from the Latin name Prudentia, "provident."

Prue, diminutive of Prudence or Prunella.

Prunella, from Latin, "plum." A 19th-century coinage.

Psyche, "soul," Greek.

Queen, from Old English, a royal title.

Queena, Old English, "queen."

Queenie, affectionate form of Queen.

Quinella, variation of Quinta.

Quinetta, variation of Quinta.

Quinn, originally an Irish surname meaning "leader."

Quinta, "fifth," Latin.

Quintessa, variation of Quinta.

Quintina, "fifth," Latin.

Rachael, variation of Rachel.

Rachel, "ewe," Hebrew. In the Old Testament, the wife of Jacob and mother of Joseph and Benjamin.

Rachelle, modern blend of Rachel and Rochelle.

Rachida, "wise," Arabic.

Rae, feminine form of Ray, or short form of Rachel.

Raelene, modern Australian coinage based on Rae and the suffix "-ene."

Raewyn, Raewynne, modern coinages based on Rae and Wynne.

Rafael, variation of Raphael.

Rafaela, variation of Raphaela.

Raina, variation of Raine.

Raine, of uncertain origin, possibly a variation of Reine.

Ramona, Spanish feminine form of Ramon, from Old German, "advice" and "protector."

Raphael, "God has healed," Hebrew. One of the archangels. Originally a boy's name.

Raphaela, feminine form of Raphael.

Raquel, Spanish form of Rachel.

Rasheeda, Rashida, variations of Rachida.

Raven, from the name of the bird, Old English.

Ray, Raye, diminutives of Raymonda or Rachel.

Raymonda, feminine form of Raymond, meaning "advice" and "protector," Old German.

Reanna, variation of Rheanna.

Reba, modern coinage based on Rebecca.

Rebecca, Rebekah, "yoke," Hebrew. In the Old Testament, the wife of Isaac and mother of Esau and Jacob.

Regan, originally an Irish surname. One of the daughters in *King Lear*.

Regina, "queen," Latin. Originally used as a personal name in the third century.

Reine, "queen," French.

Relda, New Zealand derivative of Carol.

Rena, diminutive of names such as Serena.

Renata, "reborn," Latin.

Rene, diminutive of Irene, or a variation of Renee.

Renee, "reborn," French.

Renie, diminutive of Irene.

Rewa, "tall, slender," Polynesian.

Rhea, "earth," from Greek. In Greek mythology, the mother of Zeus.

Rheanna, modern coinage based on Rhiannon and Deanna.

Rhiannon, "great queen," Welsh. A name found in Celtic mythology.

Rhoda, from Greek, "rose," or "woman from Rhodes."

Rhona, modern blend of Rose and Anna, or a diminutive of Rhonwen or Rowena.

Rhonda, Welsh, possibly from a place name meaning "powerful river" or from "lance" and "good."

Rhonwen, derived from the words for "lance" and "fair," Welsh, or "white skirt," Celtic.

Ria, diminutive of names such as Maria or Victoria, or a variation of Rhea. Also Spanish, "small river."

Rica, diminutive of Erica or Frederica.

Ricki, Rickie, Ricky, originally diminutives of Richard, "strong ruler," Old French. Also short forms of names such as Erica.

Rika, diminutive of Erika or Frederika.

Rikki, variation of Ricki.

Rima, "rhyme," Spanish, or "five," New Zealand Maori.

Rina, short form of names ending: "-rina."

Riona, "queen," Irish Gaelic.

Rita, short form of Marguerita, or from Sanskrit meaning "brave, honest."

Riva, "river bank," from French.

Roanna, "sweet," "gracious," Latin.

Robbie, Robby, short forms of Roberta.

Roberta, feminine form of Robert, "fame" and "bright," Old German.

Robin, originally an affectionate short form of Robert, its use as a girl's name is also influenced by the name of the bird.

Robyn, feminine form of Robin.

Rochella, variation of Rochelle.

Rochelle, "little rock," French.

Rochette, variation of Rochelle.

Roderica, feminine form of Roderick, from Old German, "fame" and "rule."

Rohana, blend of Rose and Hannah.

Rolanda, feminine form of Roland, "famous in the land," Old German.

Roma, Italian name for the city of Rome.

Romaine, French form of Romana.

Romana, "from Rome," Latin.

Rona, from the Scottish island of Rona, or a variation of Rhona.

Ronalda, feminine form of Ronald, "power," Old Norse.

Ronnie, Ronny, diminutives of Veronica.

Rosa, Spanish and Italian form of Rose.

Rosabel, variation of Rosa.

Rosabella, variation of Rosa.

Rosabelle, variation of Rosa.

Rosaleen, Irish form of Rosa.

Rosalia, from the Latin name for a ceremony in which rose garlands are hung on tombs.

Rosalie, French form of Rosalia.

Rosalind, from the Old German words for "horse" and "serpent." Popularized in literature as the heroine of Shakespeare's *As You Like It.*

Rosalinda, Spanish variation of Rosalind.

Rosaline, variation of Rosalind.

Rosamond, French form of Rosamund.

Rosamund, Old German, "horse" and "protection," or Latin, "pure and clean rose."

Rosana, Rosanna, variations of Roseanna.

Rose, from the name of the flower, or from Old German, "horse."

Roseanna, modern blend of Rose and Anna.

Roseanne, modern blend of Rose and Anne.

Rosemarie, German and Scandinavian form of Rosemary.

Rosemary, 18th-century blend of Rose and Mary. Also from the herb name, meaning "sea dew."

Rosetta, diminutive of Rose.

Rosie, diminutive of Rose.

Rosina, Italian diminutive of Rosa.

Rosita, Spanish diminutive of Rosa.

Roslyn, variation of Rosalind.

Rowan, "little red one," Irish Gaelic, or from the name of the tree.

Rowena, from the Old English words for "fame" and "joy."

Roxana, from Persian, "dawn." The wife of Alexander the Great.

Roxanne, variation of Roxana.

Rozalyn, variation of Rosalind.

Rozanne, variation of Roseanne.

Ruby, "red," Latin. The name of a gemstone.

Rudi, Rudy, affectionate short form of Rudolf, "famous wolf," Old German.

Rue, "fame," Old German.

Rula, Polish name, from Middle English, "ruler."

Ruth, "companion," Hebrew. In the Old Testament, the devoted daughter of Naomi.

Saba, "woman of Sheba," from Greek.

Sabina, Irish form of Sabine.

Sabine, "woman of the Sabines," an ancient Italian race.

Sabrina, the Roman name of the River Severn. In Celtic legend, a river goddess.

Sacha, French form of Sasha.

Sadie, originally an affectionate form of Sarah.

Saffron, from the name of the plant, spice, or color.

Sage, from the name of the herb, or the word meaning "wise."

Sahara, from the name of the desert.

Sahrifa, "distinguished," African.

Sally, Sallie, diminutives of Sarah.

Salome, "peace," from Hebrew. In the Bible, the step-daughter of Herod who asked for John the Baptist's head on a plate.

Sam, short form of Samantha or Samuela.

Samantha, a modern coinage.

Samuela, feminine form of Samuel, "name of God," Hebrew.

Sandie, diminutive of Sandra or Alexandra.

Sandra, Italian short form of Alessandra.

Sandy, diminutive of Sandra or Alexandra.

Sapphira, variation of Sapphire.

Sapphire, from the name of the gemstone, Greek.

Sara, variation of Sarah.

Sarah, "princess," Hebrew. In the Old Testament, the wife of Abraham and mother of Isaac. Originally called Sarai, she was ordered by God to change her name to Sarah.

Sarai, "contentious," Hebrew.

Sarina, variation of Sarah.

Sarita, variation of Sarah.

Sarra, variation of Sarah.

Sasha, Russian diminutive of Alexandra.

Savannah, from Spanish, "treeless plain." Also a river and city in Georgia.

Savina, variation of Sabine.

Scarlett, from Old French, a surname for a "fabric-seller." Popularized by the heroine of *Gone with the Wind*.

Secunda, "second," Latin.

Selena, variation of Celine.

Selene, variation of Celine.

Selima, feminine form of Solomon, "peace," Hebrew.

Selina, variation of Celine.

Selma, "fair," Celtic.

Senga, Scottish name, possibly coined from Agnes spelt backwards.

Septima, "seventh," Latin.

Serafine, variation of Seraphina.

Seraphina, "burning ones," from Hebrew. An order of angels.

Serena, "calm," from Latin.

Shae, modern variation of Shea.

Shaina, "beautiful," Hebrew.

Shana, variation of Shanna, or a feminine form of Shane.

Shaniqua, modern African-American coinage.

Shanna, modern coinage based on Shannon.

Shannon, "ancient god." The name of a river in Ireland.

Shari, diminutive of Sharon.

Sharman, variation of Charmian.

Sharon, modern coinage, based on a biblical place name meaning "flat area," Hebrew.

Shauna, feminine form of the Irish name Sean, from Hebrew, "Jehovah has favored."

Shawn, feminine form of Sean.

Shawna, feminine form of Sean.

Shea, originally an Irish surname, possibly derived from the words for "fire" and "goodly."

Sheba, diminutive of Bathsheba.

Sheena, from Sine, the Irish Gaelic form of Jane.

Sheila, Shelagh, from Sile, the Irish Gaelic form of Cecilia.

Shelby, originally a surname referring to a "village on a ledge," Old English.

Shelley, originally a surname. Used as a personal name in honor of poet Percy Bysshe Shelley.

Shelly, variation of Shelley.

Shena, from Sine, the Irish Gaelic form of Jane.

Sheree, variation of Cherie.

Sheridan, originally an Irish surname.

Sherie, variation of Cherie.

Sherilyn, modern blend of Sherry and Marilyn.

Sherri, variation of Cherie.

Sherrill, variation of Sheryl.

Sherry, variation of Cherie.

Sheryl, modern coinage from Sherry and possibly Beryl.

Shirley, originally a surname referring to someone from a "bright forest clearing," Old English.

Shona, Shonagh, Gaelic feminine forms of John, from Hebrew, "Jehovah has favored."

Shoshana, variation of Susan.

Shula, short form of the Jewish name Shulamit, "peacefulness," Hebrew.

Sian, Welsh form of Jane.

Sibyl, the name given to the women who spoke the prophecies of the ancient oracles.

Sibylla, variation of Sibyl.

Sidney, originally a surname referring to the French town St. Denis, or from Old English, "wide meadow."

Sidony, Latin feminine form of Sidonius, meaning "man from Sidon."

Siena, from the name of an Italian city.

Sierra, "mountain range," Spanish.

Signey, Signy, from the Old Norse words for "victory" and "new."

Sigourney, of uncertain origin, possibly related to a French surname meaning "senior tenant."

Sigrid, Old French personal name derived from the words for "victory" and "fair."

Sile, original Irish Gaelic spelling of Sheila, from Cecilia.

Silver, from the name of the precious metal, Old English.

Silvia, from Latin, "wood." In Roman mythology, the mother of the twins who founded Rome.

Simone, French feminine form of Simon, "hearkening," Hebrew.

Sine, original Irish Gaelic spelling of Sheena, from Jane.

Sinead, Irish Gaelic form of Janet.

Siobhan, Irish Gaelic form of Jane.

Sissie, Sissy, affectionate forms of Cecilia.

Sky, from the vocabulary word, Old Norse.

Skye, variation of Sky, or from the name of the Scottish island.

Sofia, Swedish form of Sophia.

Sofie, Dutch form of Sophia.

Sondra, variation of Sandra.

Sonia, Sonja, Sonya, Russian affectionate forms of Sophia.

Sophia, "wisdom," Greek.

Sophie, French and German form of Sophia.

Sosanna, variation of Susan.

Spring, from the name of the season, Old English.

Stacey, Stacy, short forms of Anastasia or Eustacia.

Star, Starr, from the vocabulary word, in modern usage as a name.

Stefanie, Stefany, variations of Stephanie.

Steffi, Steffy, affectionate short forms of Stephanie.

Stella, "star," Latin.

Stephanie, French feminine form of Stephen, "crown," Greek.

Stevie, affectionate short form of Stephanie.

Sue, short form of Susan.

Summer, from the name of the season, Old English.

Susan, "lily," Hebrew.

Susanna, Susannah, biblical forms of Susan.

Susie, affectionate form of Susan.

Suzanna, Suzannah, variations of Susanna.

Suzanne, French form of Susan.

Suzette, French affectionate form of Suzanne.

Suzy, diminutive of Susan.

Sybil, variation of Sibyl.

Sydney, variation of Sidney. Also a place name.

Sylva, variation of Silvia.

Sylvia, variation of Silvia.

Sylvie, French form of Silvia.

Tabby, Tabbie, Tabbi, affectionate short forms of Tabitha.

Tabitha, "gazelle," Aramaic. In the New Testament, a woman restored to life by St. Peter.

Tace, medieval personal name, "be silent," Latin.

Tacita, feminine form of a Roman family name, from Latin, "silent."

Tacy, Tacye, variations of Tace.

Tahne, "desirable," Native American.

Talia, "plentiful," Greek, or short form of Natalia.

Talitha, "little girl," Aramaic.

Tallulah, "running water," Native American, or a variation of Talulla.

Talulla, from the Irish Gaelic words for "abundance" and "princess."

Talya, short form of Natalya.

Tamar, "palm tree," Hebrew.

Tamara, Russian form of Tamar.

Tammy, Tammie, affectionate forms of Tamara or Tamsin.

Tamsin, variation of Thomasina.

Taneisha, Tanesha, Taneshia, variations of Tanisha.

Tania, diminutive of Tatiana.

Tanisha, "born on Monday," African.

Tanith, the Carthaginian goddess of love.

Tansy, from the plant name, "immortality," Old French, from Greek.

Tanya, Russian diminutive of Tatiana.

Tara, "hill," Irish Gaelic. A place in Ireland believed to be the seat of high kings.

Tariro, "to hope," African.

Tasha, short form of Natasha.

Tatiana, Russian personal name, from a Roman family name.

Tatum, "Tate's homestead," Old English.

Taylor, originally an Old English surname referring to a "tailor" by trade.

Teal, a color name.

Teddy, affectionate short form of Edwina or Theodora.

Tempest, modern coinage as a name, meaning "storm."

Teresa, Italian and Spanish form of Theresa.

Terri, Teri, affectionate short forms of Theresa.

Tess, affectionate short form of Theresa.

Tessa, affectionate short form of Theresa.

Thalia, the muse of comedy in Greek mythology, meaning "to flourish."

Thea, short form of Dorothea or Althea.

Thecla, variation of Thekla.

Theda, short form of a number of Old German personal names derived from the word for "people."

Thekla, from the Greek words for "god" and "famous," dating to the first century.

Thelma, from Greek meaning "wish" or "will." Coined in the 19th century for a novel.

Thena, variation of Athena.

Theodora, feminine form of Theodore, from Greek, "god" and "gift."

Theodosia, Greek name derived from "god" and "giving."

Thera, "wild," Greek.

Theresa, of uncertain origin, possibly related to the Greek island of Thera.

Therese, French form of Theresa.

Thomasa, feminine form of Thomas, "twin," Aramaic.

Thomasin, feminine form of Thomas.

Thomasina, feminine form of Thomas.

Thyra, "dedicated to Tyr," referring to the god of war, Old Norse.

Tia, short form of names such as Letitia.

Tiara, modern coinage based on the Latin word for "headdress."

Tierra, "earth," Spanish.

Tiffany, medieval personal name. From Greek, "god appears."

Tilly, affectionate form of Matilda.

Timothea, feminine form of Timothy, "honor god," Greek.

Tina, short form of names such as Christina or Martina.

Tirion, "kind, gentle," Welsh personal name.

Tirzah, "pleasant," "delight," Hebrew.

Tisha, diminutive of Letitia.

Toni, short form of Antonia or feminine form of Tony.

Tonia, Tonya, short forms of Antonia.

Tori, affectionate short form of Victoria.

Toval, "good," Hebrew.

Tracey, Tracy, originally a surname and boy's name. Derived from the Roman personal name Thracius.

Tricia, diminutive of Patricia.

Trina, Trena, short form of Katrina.

Trinity, from the name of the three aspects of God: the Father, the Son and the Holy Ghost.

Trisha, Trish, diminutive of Patricia.

Trixie, diminutive of Beatrix.

Trudy, Trudie, "strength," Old German. Affectionate short forms of names such as Gertrude.

Tryphena, "delicate," Greek.

Tuesday, from the day of the week.

Tui, the name of a bird, New Zealand Maori.

Twyla, "woven of double thread," Middle English.

Tyler, "tile-maker," Old English surname.

Tyne, "flowing," Celtic. The name of an English river.

Ula, "jewel of the sea," Celtic.

Ulla, short form of Ursula.

Ulrica, feminine form of Ulric, from Old Norse, "wolf" and "ruler."

Uma, "flax," "turmeric," Sanskrit. A goddess considered to be the epitome of good speech.

Una, "one," Latin. Also a name originating in medieval Ireland.

Unity, from the vocabulary word, Latin.

Ursa, short form of Ursula.

Ursula, "female bear," Latin.

Uta, diminutive of Ottalie.

Val, short form of Valerie.

Valda, modern coinage based on Val.

Valentina, variation of Valentine.

Valentine, "strong, healthy," Latin.

Valeria, Italian form of Valerie.

Valerie, French form of an Old Roman family name meaning "healthy."

Valery, variation of Valerie.

Valetta, modern coinage based on Val.

Valmai, "mayflower," Welsh.

Vanda, variation of Wanda.

Vanessa, invented by Jonathan Swift in the 18th century for his friend Esther Vanhomrigh, using some of the syllables from her name.

Vanetta, feminine form of Van.

Varda, "rose," Hebrew.

Venetia, possibly derived from the Latin name of the Italian city Venice.

Venice, from the name of the Italian city.

Ventura, "venture," Latin.

Venus, the Roman goddess of love.

Vera, "faith," a Russian personal name.

Verena, a Swiss personal name of uncertain origin, dating to the third century.

Verity, "truth," Latin.

Verna, modern coinage, possibly from Latin, "of spring."

Verona, from the name of the Italian city, or a short form of Veronica.

Veronica, Latin form of Berenice. Associated with the Latin phrase "vera icon," meaning "true image," referring to the image of Christ.

Veronique, French form of Veronica.

Vesta, the Roman goddess of the hearth.

Vi, short form of Violet.

Vicky, Vickie, Vicki, short forms of Victoria.

Victoria, feminine form of a Latin name meaning "victory."

Vienna, from the name of the Austrian city.

Vikki, Vikky, short forms of Victoria.

Viola, an Italian personal name, from the Latin word for "violet."

Violet, from the name of the flower, Latin.

Violetta, variation of Viola or Violet.

Virginia, feminine form of a Roman family name, possibly derived from the Latin word for "virgin."

Virginie, French form of Virginia.

Vita, "life," Latin.

Vivian, "alive," Latin. Originally a boy's name.

Vivien, feminine form of Vivian.

Vivienne, French feminine form of Vivian.

Wanda, from Old German, "stem," or Australian Aboriginal, "sandhills."

Wenda, modern coinage based on Wendy.

Wendy, invented for the character of Wendy Darling in *Peter Pan*.

Whitley, originally a surname referring to a place name.

Whitney, originally a surname referring to a place, "white island."

Wilhelmina, German feminine form of William, "will" and "protect," Old German.

Willa, modern coinage based on William.

Williamina, feminine form of William.

Willow, from the name of the tree, Old English.

Wilma, short form of Wilhelmina.

Wilmette, modern coinage based on Wilma.

Winifred, English form of a Welsh personal name, derived from the words for "white" or "blessed" and "reconciliation."

Winona, "first-born daughter," Sioux.

Wynne, short form of Winifred, from Welsh, "fair." Also "friend," Old English.

Wynonna, variation of Winona.

X

Xanthe, "yellow, bright," from Greek.

Xaviera, feminine form of Xavier, "new house," Spanish.

Xenia, "hospitality," Greek.

Y

Yasmin, Arabic variation of Jasmine.

Yoko, "good," Japanese.

Yolanda, variation of Yolande.

Yolande, Old French personal name of uncertain origin, possibly derived from Viola.

Ysanne, modern coinage based on Yseult or Yvonne and Anne.

Yseult, medieval French form of Isolde.

Yvette, French feminine diminutive of Yvon, "yew," Old German.

Yvonne, French feminine diminutive of Yvon.

Z

Zabrina, variation of Sabrina.

Zandra, variation of Sandra.

Zanna, modern coinage, possibly based on Suzanna.

Zara, of uncertain origin, possibly a variation of Sara, or from Arabic, "flower."

Zelah, "side," Hebrew. An Old Testament name.

Zelda, modern coinage based on Griselda.

Zelma, variation of Selma.

Zena, of uncertain origin, possibly from Persian, "woman."

Zenobia, "father's ornament," Greek.

Zephyrine, "west wind," French, from Greek.

Zeta, of uncertain origin, possibly a variation of Zita.

Zia, "tremble," Hebrew.

Zillah, "shade," Hebrew. An Old Testament name.

Zinnia, from the name of the flower.

Zita, possibly derived from a medieval Tuscan nickname, "girl."

Zoe, "life," Greek.

Zola, modern coinage, possibly based on Zoe, or derived from a surname.

Zora, variation of Aurora.

Zsa Zsa, Hungarian affectionate form of Susan.

Zula, modern coinage based on the Zulu tribe.

Boys' Names

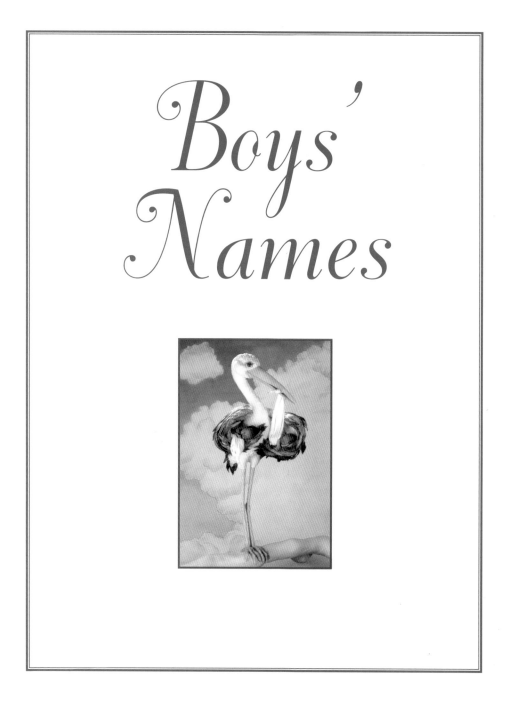

Aaro, variation of Aaron.

Aaron, of uncertain origin, possibly Hebrew, meaning "high mountain."

Abbot, Abbott, Old English, the name of the head of an abbey. From Aramaic, "father."

Abe, short form of Abraham.

Abel, "breath," Hebrew. The first murder victim mentioned in the Old Testament.

Abner, "father of light," Hebrew.

Abraham, "father of many," Hebrew. In the Old Testament, Abram was chosen to found the Hebrew nation and his name was changed to Abraham.

Ace, synonymous now with "the best," from Latin, "unit."

Achilles, a legendary Greek warrior killed by an arrow in his heel, his only vulnerable spot.

Acton, originally a surname meaning "from the town near the oaks," Old English.

Adair, Scottish form of Edgar.

Adam, "from the earth," Hebrew. The first man in the Bible.

Adamo, Italian form of Adam.

Adan, Spanish form of Adam.

Addison, "son of Adam," Old English.

Adlai, short form of the Old Testament name Adaliah, "God is just," Hebrew.

Adler, "eagle," Old German.

Adrian, "from Hadria," Latin.

Adrien, French form of Adrian.

Aharon, modern Hebrew form of Aaron.

Ahmed, "praiseworthy," Arabic.

Aidan, "little fire," Irish Gaelic.

Aiken, "little Adam," Old English.

Ainsley, Ainslie, originally a Scottish surname meaning "meadow."

Akeem, variation of Hakeem.

Al, short form of names such as Alan.

Alan, ancient Celtic name derived from the words for "spirit" and "rock."

Alasdair, Scottish Gaelic form of Alexander.

Alastair, English variation of Alasdair.

Alban, "from Alba," Latin. The first martyr of Roman Britain.

Albert, from an Old German personal name derived from the words for "noble" and "bright."

Alberto, Spanish and Italian form of Albert.

Albion, "white," Latin.

Albrecht, German form of Albert.

Aldo, from an Old German name derived from the words for "old" and "wise."

Aldous, variation of Aldo.

Aldred, "old counsel," Old English.

Alec, Scottish diminutive of Alexander.

Aled, "offspring," Welsh.

Alex, diminutive of Alexander.

Alexander, "defender of men," Greek, after Alexander the Great.

Alexis, variation of Alexander.

Alf, short form of Alfred or Alfonso.

Alfie, diminutive of Alfred or Alfonso.

Alfonso, "noble and eager," from Old German. A popular name for Spanish royalty.

Alfred, from an Old English personal name derived from the words for "elf" and "counsel."

Alfredo, Spanish or Italian form of Alfred.

Algernon, "whiskered," Old French.

Ali, "exalted," Arabic.

Alisdair, variation of Alasdair.

Alistair, variation of Alasdair.

Allan, Allen, Allyn, variations of Alan.

Aloysius, Provençal form of Louis.

Alphonse, French form of Alfonso.

Alton, "old town," Old English.

Alvin, "elf friend," Old English.

Alvis, possibly from Old Norse, "all wise."

Alwin, Alwyn, variations of Alvin.

Amadeus, "lover of god," Latin.

Ambrose, "immortal," Greek.

Amir, "local prince," Arabic.

Amory, "famous ruler," Teutonic.

Amos, "to carry," Hebrew. An Old Testament prophet.

Anatole, "from the east," from Greek.

Anatoly, Russian form of Anatole.

Anderson, "son of Andrew," originally an English surname.

Andre, French form of Andrew.

Andreas, German form of Andrew.

Andres, Spanish form of Andrew.

Andrew, "warrior," Greek. One of the 12 disciples in the New Testament, and the patron saint of Scotland and Russia.

Andy, affectionate short form of Andrew.

Angel, Spanish form of Angelo.

Angelo, "messenger," Italian, from Latin.

Angus, "one choice," from Gaelic. Aengus was the Celtic god of love.

Ansel, variation of Anselm.

Anselm, derived from the Old German words for "god" and "helmet."

Anson, "Anne's son," Old English.

Anthony, from Latin, "worthy of praise."

Antoine, French form of Anthony.

Antonio, Italian and Spanish form of Anthony.

Antony, variation of Anthony.

Aram, "height," Hebrew. A biblical name.

Archer, "bowman," Old English.

Archibald, derived from the Old German words for "genuine" and "brave."

Ari, variation of Arye.

Ariel, "lion of God," Hebrew, from the biblical place name. The sprite in Shakespeare's *The Tempest*, and in Israel, a common boy's name.

Aristo, "best," Greek short form of Aristophanes or Aristotle.

Arlow, "fortified town," from Old English.

Armand, French form of Hermann.

Armando, Spanish form of Hermann.

Armin, German variation of Hermann.

Arnie, diminutive of Arnold.

Arnold, medieval name derived from the Old German words for "eagle" and "ruler."

Aron, variation of Aaron.

Art, diminutive of Arthur.

Artemas, Greek name from the New Testament, possibly related to the Greek goddess Artemis.

Arthur, ancient name of uncertain origin, possibly Celtic, "bear," or from Irish, "stone." Associated with the legendary King Arthur of the Round Table.

Arye, "lion," Hebrew.

Asa, "physician," Hebrew. An Old Testament name, the King of Judah.

Ash, short form of Ashley.

Asher, "happy," Hebrew.

Ashley, Ashleigh, Old English, originally a surname referring to "ash wood."

Ashton, originally an Old English surname meaning "settlement."

Auberon, diminutive of Aubrey.

Aubrey, from German, "elf power."

August, variation of Augustus.

Augustus, "magnificent," Latin. An Old Roman name used as a title by the emperors.

Austin, Austen, medieval forms of the personal name Augustus, later surviving as a surname.

Averil, Averill, Averell, from Old English, "boar" and "battle."

Avery, from the surname, a variation of Alfred.

Avi, short form of a number of Hebrew names.

Axel, Danish form of Absalom, a Hebrew name meaning "father of peace."

Azis, "mighty," Arabic.

Bailey, originally a surname from the Middle Ages referring to a "bailiff."

Baillie, variation of Bailey.

Baird, "minstrel," Celtic.

Baldwin, from the surname, derived from a Norman personal name meaning "brave friend."

Balthasar, Balthazar, Greek forms of an Old Testament name meaning "Baal protect the king."

Barclay, Scottish surname derived from the Old English words for "birch tree" and "wood."

Barden, "barley valley," Old English surname.

Barnabas, "son of consolation," Hebrew. From the New Testament.

Barnaby, medieval form of Barnabas.

Barney, affectionate short form of Barnabas.

Barry, English form of an Irish Gaelic name derived from the word for "spear."

Bart, diminutive of Bartholomew.

Bartholomew, "son of Talmai," Aramaic. From the New Testament.

Barton, originally an Old English surname, a diminutive of Bartholomew.

Bartram, variation of Bertram.

Basil, "royal," Greek. The founder of the Eastern Orthodox Church.

Baxter, from the Middle Ages, a surname referring to a baker by trade.

Bayard, "red-headed," Old English.

Bayley, variation of Bailey.

Baynard, variation of Bayard.

Beau, originally a nickname meaning "handsome," French. The name of a character in *Gone with the Wind*.

Beaumont, "beautiful mountain," French.

Ben, short form of Benedict or Benjamin.

Benedick, variation of Benedict. The name given to a confirmed bachelor who marries, as in Shakespeare's *Much Ado About Nothing*.

Benedict, "blessed," Latin.

Benjamin, "son of my right hand," Hebrew. In the Old Testament, the youngest son of Jacob.

Bennett, from the surname, originally a variation of Benedict.

Benny, diminutive of Benjamin.

Benson, from the English surname, "son of Ben."

Bentley, Old English surname referring to the "farm where the grass bends."

Benton, variation of Bentley.

Bern, short form of Bernard.

Bernard, "brave as a bear," from Old German. St. Bernard is the patron saint of mountaineers.

Bernie, diminutive of Bernard.

Bert, short form of names such as Albert and Bertram.

Bertie, diminutive of names such as Albert and Bertram.

Bertram, Old German, "bright raven," a symbol of wisdom in German mythology.

Bertrand, French variation of Bertram.

Bevan, "son of Evan," Welsh.

Bevis, possibly from Old French, "dear son," or referring to the place name Beauvais.

Bill, diminutive of William.

Billy, Billie, diminutives of William.

Bing, originally a surname referring to a place, "clearing with a hollow." Popularized by singer Bing Crosby.

Bjorn, "bear," Old Norse.

Blain, Blaine, possibly derived from the Gaelic word for "yellow," or from Old English "flaming."

Blair, originally a Scottish Gaelic surname signifying "from the plain."

Blaise, "lisping," from Latin. A popular name in France.

Blake, surname derived from the Old English words for "black" and "pale."

Blakely, variation of Blake.

Blane, variation of Blain.

Bo, "householder," Old Norse. A popular Scandinavian personal name.

Boaz, from Hebrew, "swift." An Old Testament name.

Bob, diminutive of Robert.

Bobby, Bobbie, diminutives of Robert.

Bogart, "strong bow," Old French.

Boris, short form of the Russian name Borislav, "battle glory."

Boston, place name in recent usage as a personal name.

Bowie, "yellow-haired," Irish Gaelic.

Boyd, "yellow-haired," Scottish Gaelic.

Brad, "broad," Old English, a diminutive of Bradford or Bradley.

Braden, originally a surname derived from the Gaelic word for "salmon."

Bradford, originally a surname signifying someone from the "broad ford," Old English.

Bradley, originally a surname referring to someone from the "broad meadow."

Brady, originally an Irish Gaelic surname meaning "spirited one."

Bram, short form of Abraham.

Brandon, originally an Old English surname, a variation of Brendan.

Brendan, Brendon, "prince," Celtic. In legend, St. Brendan was reputed to have discovered the New World.

Brennan, Brennen, "drop of water," Irish Gaelic surname.

Brent, originally a surname, from the Old English words for "high" or "burnt."

Brett, Bret, originally an ethnic name for a Breton or Briton.

Brian, Celtic name from the words for "high" and "noble." The High King of Ireland in the 10th century.

Brice, "son of Rhys," Celtic.

Brock, originally a surname meaning "badger," Old English.

Broderick, Welsh name meaning "son of Roderick."

Bronson, Old English, "son of the dark-skinned man."

Brown, from the name of the color.

Bruce, of uncertain origin. A prominent Scottish surname, borne notably by Robert the Bruce, who ruled Scotland in the 14th century.

Bruno, "brown," Old German.

Bryan, variation of Brian.

Bryant, variation of Brian.

Bryce, variation of Brice.

Bryn, "hill," Welsh.

Brynmor, "large hill," Welsh.

Bryson, originally a surname, "son of Bryce."

Burgess, originally a surname, "freeman," Old French.

Burl, short form of Burleigh.

Burleigh, from the Old English words for "fort" and "meadow."

Burt, short form of Burton.

Burton, originally a surname meaning "fortified settlement," Old English.

Byron, originally a surname referring to "cattlesheds," Old English. Used as a personal name in honor of the English poet Byron.

Caesar, "long-haired," Latin, later meaning "emperor."

Cain, "spear," Hebrew. In the Bible, the first murderer. He killed his brother Abel.

Cale, short form of Caleb.

Caleb, "bold," Hebrew.

Callum, Calum, "devotee of St. Columba," Scottish Gaelic.

Calvin, "bald," Latin.

Cameron, "crooked nose," Scottish Gaelic.

Campbell, "crooked mouth," Scottish Gaelic.

Cane, variation of Cain.

Carl, Old German form of Charles.

Carleton, variation of Charlton.

Carlos, Spanish form of Carl.

Carlton, variation of Charlton.

Carrick, from the Gaelic words for "rock" or "cliff."

Carroll, "champion warrior," Celtic.

Carson, originally a surname, "son of a marsh-dweller," Old English.

Carter, originally an Old English surname referring to a "cart-driver."

Cary, originally a surname referring to an Old Celtic river name.

Casey, "vigilant," Irish Gaelic.

Caspar, Dutch form of Jasper. One of the three wise men who brought gifts to Jesus in the New Testament.

Casper, variation of Caspar.

Cassidy, of uncertain meaning, originally an Irish surname.

Cassius, from a Roman family name meaning "hollow," Latin.

Cato, "knowledge," Latin.

Cecil, from an Old Roman family name meaning "blind," Latin.

Cedric, coined by Sir Walter Scott in the novel *Ivanhoe.*

Cesar, French form of Caesar.

Chad, from Old English, possibly meaning "battle."

Chadwick, originally a surname referring to someone from a dairy farm, Old English.

Chaim, "life," Hebrew.

Chance, originally a surname for someone who had good fortune, Old English.

Chandler, Old English surname referring to a "candlemaker" by trade.

Charles, from Old German, "freeman." Popularized by Charles the Great, the ruler of the Holy Roman Empire in the ninth century.

Charlie, Charley, diminutives of Charles.

Charlton, originally a surname, "from the town of freemen," Old English.

Chase, "hunter," Old French.

Chauncy, "record-keeper," Old French.

Chester, originally a surname referring to someone from the town of Chester.

Chevy, from Chevalier, "knight," Old French.

Chioke, "gift of god," African.

Chris, short form of Christopher.

Christian, "follower of Christ," Latin.

Christoph, German form of Christopher.

Christophe, French form of Christopher.

Christopher, "bearer of Christ," Greek. The patron saint of travelers.

Chuck, diminutive of Charles.

Churchill, originally a surname referring to someone from the "church hill," Old English.

Cian, "ancient," Irish Gaelic.

Ciaran, "black," Irish Gaelic.

Clancy, "ruddy warrior," Irish.

Clarence, the name of a dukedom in England, from Latin, "illustrious, prominent."

Clark, Clarke, originally surnames referring to a cleric by profession.

Claud, variation of Claude.

Claude, French form of Claudius.

Claudius, from the Roman family name meaning "lame," Latin.

Clay, originally a surname, Old English, "from the clay."

Clayton, Old English surname referring to the "settlement on the clay."

Cleanth, from a Greek family name.

Clem, short form of Clement.

Clement, "mild, gentle," Latin.

Cleon, "famous," Greek. The Athenian leader in the Peloponnesian war.

Cleve, short form of Cleveland.

Cleveland, "cliff land," Old English. Used as a personal name in honor of U.S. President Grover Cleveland.

Cliff, short form of Clifford.

Clifford, originally an Old English surname referring to someone from the "settlement by the slope."

Clifton, Old English surname referring to the "town near the cliff."

Clint, short form of Clinton.

Clinton, Old English surname referring to someone from the "town on the hill."

Clive, from the Old English place name meaning "cliff." Originally a surname.

Clovis, Latinized form of Louis.

Clyde, from the name of the Scottish river.

Cody, originally an Irish surname referring to a "helpful person."

Col, medieval short form of Nicholas.

Colby, "Koli's farm," Old Norse, Koli being a nickname for a swarthy person.

Cole, from Old English, "coal-black." Also a diminutive of Nicholas.

Colin, diminutive of Col, a short form of Nicholas.

Colm, "dove," Irish Gaelic, from Latin.

Colman, English surname based on Colm.

Colton, "town where colts are bred," Old English.

Colum, variation of Colm.

Conall, Old Celtic name derived from the words for "wolf" and "strong."

Conan, "high," Celtic.

Conell, variation of Conall.

Conn, "chief," Old Celtic. Also a short form of Connor.

Connor, Conor, "lover of hounds," Irish Gaelic.

Conrad, from Old German, "bold counsel."

Constantine, from Latin, "constant."

Cooper, originally a surname for a "barrel-maker" by trade, Old English.

Corbin, "raven," Old French.

Corey, "from the hollow," Irish Gaelic.

Cormac, Irish Gaelic, from the words for "defilement" and "son."

Cornelius, Old Roman family name meaning "horn," Latin.

Cornell, medieval form of Cornelius.

Cory, variation of Corey.

Cosimo, variation of Cosmo.

Cosmo, "order, beauty," Greek.

Courtney, Courtenay, Courteney, originally a surname referring to Courtenay, the name of several places in France.

Cowal, English form of an Irish personal name.

Craig, originally a surname meaning "rock," Scottish Gaelic.

Crispian, medieval variation of Crispin.

Crispin, from a Roman family name meaning "curly-haired." St. Crispin is the patron saint of shoemakers.

Cristian, variation of Christian.

Crosby, "from the crossroads," an Old English surname.

Cullen, originally a surname meaning "handsome," Irish Gaelic.

Curt, diminutive of Conrad, or a short form of Curtis.

Curtis, originally a surname meaning "courteous," Old French.

Cy, short form of Cyril or Cyrus.

Cyprian, "native of Cyprus," Latin.

Cyrano, "from Cyrene," Greek.

Cyril, Cyrille, "lord," Greek.

Cyrus, "lord," Greek. The name of several kings of Persia.

Dakota, from the name of the Native American nation and the place name.

Dale, originally a surname referring to someone from the "valley."

Daley, Irish Gaelic surname meaning "gathering."

Dallas, possibly from Gaelic, "wise." A city in Texas.

Dalton, surname meaning "farm in the valley."

Damian, Damien, from Greek, "divine power" or "fate."

Damon, from Greek, "to tame."

Dan, "he judged," Hebrew. An Old Testament name, one of Jacob's sons. Also a short form of Daniel.

Dane, originally a surname, "from Denmark," Old English.

Daniel, "God is my judge," Hebrew. An Old Testament prophet.

Danny, Dannie, short affectionate forms of Daniel.

Dante, short form of Durante.

Danyon, variation of Daniel.

Darby, originally a surname referring to a "deer park," Old English.

Darcy, from the French place name Arcy. Brought to England during the Norman conquests.

Darin, Daren, variations of Darren.

Darius, "possessing good," a name borne by Persian kings.

Darrell, Darrel, variations of Darryl.

Darren, coined in modern times, possibly meaning "small rocky hill."

Darrin, Darron, variations of Darren.

Darryl, Daryl, once a surname referring to Airelle in France.

Dave, diminutive of David.

Davey, diminutive of David.

David, from the Old Testament Hebrew name meaning "beloved." The slayer of Goliath who became the King of Israel. The patron saint of Wales.

Davis, "son of David."

Davy, diminutive of David.

Davyd, variation of David.

Dayle, variation of Dale.

Dean, originally a surname meaning "from the valley," Old English, or from Latin, "leader."

Deandre, modern coinage from prefix "De-" and Andre.

Deane, variation of Dean.

Deangelo, modern coinage from prefix "De-" and Angelo.

Declan, Irish personal name of uncertain origin.

Dee, "holy one," Welsh, or short form of "D" names.

Dejuan, modern coinage from prefix "De-" and Juan.

Delaney, "descendant of the challenger," Irish Gaelic.

Delbert, variation of the Dutch form of Albert.

Delmar, "from the sea," Spanish.

Demarco, modern coinage from prefix "De-" and Marco.

Demarcus, modern coinage from prefix "De-" and Marcus.

Demario, modern coinage from prefix "De-" and Mario.

Demetrius, "belonging to Demeter," Demeter being the goddess of fertility.

Dempsey, "proud," Irish.

Denis, French form of Dennis. The patron saint of France.

Dennis, from Dionysius, the Greek god of wine.

Dennison, "son of Dennis," Old English.

Denny, short form of Dennis.

Denton, originally a surname referring to someone from a "valley settlement."

Denver, "from the edge of the valley," Old English.

Denzel, variation of Denzil.

Denzil, surname from Cornwall, England, meaning "high stronghold."

Derby, variation of Darby.

Derek, of uncertain meaning, from the Old German personal name Theodoric.

Dermot, Dermott, "free from envy," Old Celtic.

Derrick, variation of Derek.

Derry, diminutive of Dermot.

Desmond, originally an Irish surname meaning "man from south Munster."

Devin, variation of Devon.

Devon, originally a surname referring to the English county.

Dewey, variation of Dewi.

Dewi, Welsh form of David.

Dex, short form of Dexter.

Dexter, from Latin, "right-handed," or from Old English, referring to a "dyer" by trade.

Dick, diminutive of Richard dating from the 13th century.

Dicky, Dickie, diminutives of Richard.

Diego, Spanish form of James.

Dieter, Old German, from the words for "people" and "race."

Digby, originally an Old English surname referring to a "farm by a ditch."

Dillon, variation of Dylan.

Dimitri, variation of Dmitri.

Dion, French personal name, from Latin, "God."

Dirk, Dutch form of Derek.

Dmitri, Russian form of Demetrius.

Dominic, Dominick, "of the Lord," Latin. The founder of an order of monks in the 13th century first popularized the name.

Don, short form of Donald.

Donal, "world rule," Old Celtic.

Donald, English and Scottish form of Donal. Associated with the MacDonald clan, which ruled Scotland in medieval times.

Donnell, variation of Donal.

Donovan, originally a surname meaning "dark brown," Irish.

Doran, "stranger," Irish Gaelic.

Dorian, from Greek, the ethnic name of an ancient Greek people. First used as a personal name by Oscar Wilde in *The Picture of Dorian Gray.*

Douglas, "dark water," Scottish Gaelic. Originally a place name and a Scottish clan.

Drake, "dragon," Old English.

Drew, short form of Andrew.

Duane, "dark," Irish Gaelic.

Dudley, originally a surname borne by an English family of nobility, meaning "Dudda's clearing," Old English.

Duff, Scottish name, from a Gaelic nickname meaning "dark-haired."

Duke, short form of Marmaduke, also a noble title.

Duncan, English and Scottish variation of an Irish Gaelic name meaning "brown chief."

Dunstan, "dark stone," Old English. Patron saint of locksmiths, jewelers and the blind.

Durand, "enduring," Latin.

Durante, "lasting," Italian.

Dustin, "Thor's stone," Old Norse.

Dwain, Dwayne, variations of Duane.

Dwight, originally a surname related to Dionysius. Popularized as a first name in honor of U.S. President Dwight D. Eisenhower.

Dylan, Welsh name, possibly from Celtic, "sea."

Dylon, variation of Dylan.

Eamon, Eamonn, Irish Gaelic forms of Edmund.

Earl, Earle, from Old English, "noble warrior."

Easter, from the name of the Christian festival.

Easton, originally a surname referring to someone from an "eastern village or farm."

Eben, "stone," Hebrew. Short form of Ebenezer.

Ebenezer, "stone of help," Hebrew. The first name of Scrooge in Charles Dickens' *A Christmas Carol*.

Ed, short form of Edgar, Edward or Edmund.

Eddie, Eddy, short forms of Edgar, Edward or Edmund.

Eden, "delight," Hebrew.

Edgar, from the Old English words for "spear" and "rich."

Edison, "son of Edward," Old English. Inspired as a personal name by inventor Thomas A. Edison.

Edmund, Edmond, from the Old English words for "riches" and "protector."

Edom, Scottish variation of Adam.

Eduardo, Spanish form of Edward.

Edward, Old English personal name meaning "riches" and "guard," dating from the early Middle Ages.

Edwin, "rich friend," Old English.

Egan, "little fire," Irish Gaelic.

Egbert, Old English personal name derived from the words for "sword edge" and "bright."

Eldon, Elden, originally a surname, possibly derived from Old English, "elf valley" or "from the holy hill."

Eldred, variation of Aldred.

Eldridge, "advisor," Old English.

Eleazar, "God's helper," Hebrew. An Old Testament name.

Elfred, variation of Alfred.

Eli, "height," Hebrew. From the Old Testament.

Elias, Greek form of Elijah.

Elijah, "Jehovah is God," Hebrew. Borne by an Old Testament prophet.

Eliot, Eliott, variations of Elliot.

Elisha, Hebrew, "God is salvation."

Elizor, variation of Eleazar.

Ellery, "dweller by the elder tree," Teutonic, or from Greek, "sweetly speaking."

Elliot, Elliott, from the surname derived from the Old French version of Elias.

Ellis, variation of Elias.

Ellwood, variation of Elwood.

Elmer, originally a surname derived from an Old English personal name meaning "famous" and "noble."

Elmo, "protector," Italian, or from Greek, "friendly."

Elroy, variation of Leroy.

Elsdon, originally a surname referring to someone from "Elli's valley," Old English.

Elton, originally a surname referring to someone from "eel town" or "Ella's town."

Elvin, variation of Alvin.

Elvis, of uncertain origin. Popularized by singer Elvis Presley.

Elwood, "from the forest," Old English.

Elwyn, "fair," Welsh, or a variation of Alan.

Ely, variation of Eli.

Emanuel, Scandinavian form of Emmanuel.

Emerson, originally a surname meaning "son of Emery," Old English.

Emery, from the Old German words for "labor" and "ruler."

Emil, German and Scandinavian form of an old Roman family name. From Latin, "rival."

Emile, French form of Emil.

Emilio, Italian and Spanish form of Emil.

Emlyn, Welsh form of Emil.

Emmanuel, "God is with us," Hebrew. The name of the Messiah prophesied in the Old Testament.

Emmet, Emmett, from the surname, originally a diminutive of Emma, meaning "universal," Old German.

Emrys, Welsh form of Ambrose.

Engelbert, "bright angel," Teutonic.

Enoch, "educated," Hebrew. An Old Testament name.

Enos, "mankind," Hebrew.

Enrico, Italian form of Henry.

Enzo, originally a short form of Lorenzo or Vincenzo.

Ephraim, "fruitful," Hebrew.

Erasmus, "beloved," Greek. The patron saint of sailors.

Erhard, from the Old German words for "strong" and "resolved."

Eric, "ever ruler," Old Norse.

Erich, German form of Eric.

Erik, Swedish form of Eric.

Erin, the ancient name for Ireland.

Erl, Erle, variations of Earl.

Ernest, "serious battle," Old German.

Ernie, diminutive of Ernest.

Ernst, German form of Ernest.

Errol, Scottish surname and place name.

Erwin, derived from the Old English words for "boar" and "wine."

Esau, "hairy," Hebrew. In the Old Testament, Isaac's eldest son.

Esmond, Old English personal name derived from the words for "beauty" and "protection."

Esteban, Spanish form of Stephen.

Ethan, biblical name derived from the Hebrew words for "permanence" and "strength."

Etienne, French form of Stephen.

Euan, "a youth," Scottish Gaelic.

Eugene, "well born," Greek.

Eustace, "fruitful," Greek. Borne as early as the second century by a martyred Roman soldier.

Evan, Welsh form of John.

Everard, "strong boar," Old German.

Everett, variation of Everard.

Ewan, variation of Euan.

Ewart, originally a Scottish surname referring to a "sheep herd," or a place name.

Ewen, variation of Euan.

Ezekiel, "may God strengthen us," Hebrew. An Old Testament prophet.

Ezra, from Hebrew, "help, salvation." An Old Testament prophet.

Faber, variation of Fabian.

Fabian, originally an Old Roman family name meaning "bean-grower."

Fabio, Italian form of Fabian.

Fabron, "blacksmith," French.

Fagan, Fagin, "fiery," Gaelic.

Fairfax, "fair-headed," originally an Old English surname.

Farley, "clearing with ferns," Old English.

Faron, variation of Farron.

Farquhar, originally a Scottish Gaelic surname meaning "dear friend."

Farran, Farren, originally a surname, possibly from Old French, "pilferer" or "ferret," or a medieval form of Ferdinand.

Farrell, "brave," Irish Gaelic.

Farron, "man of courage," Greek.

Favell, "brave," Irish.

Favin, "understanding," Latin.

Fedor, variation of Theodore.

Felix, "lucky," Latin.

Felton, Old English surname referring to someone "from the town."

Fenton, originally an Old English surname referring to someone from the "settlement on the marsh."

Feodor, variation of Theodore.

Ferdinand, Spanish name of German origin, meaning "ready journey."

Fergus, derived from the Gaelic words for "vigor" and "man."

Ferguson, originally a surname, "son of Fergus."

Fernand, French form of Ferdinand.

Fernando, Spanish form of Ferdinand.

Ferris, originally an Irish surname associated with the Fergus and Ferguson clans.

Fess, short form of Festus.

Festus, "steadfast," Latin. From an Old Roman family name.

Fidel, "faithful," Spanish, from Latin.

Fife, originally a surname for someone from the Scottish kingdom of Fife.

Finlay, English form of a Scottish Gaelic name meaning "fair warrior."

Finn, "fair," Irish Gaelic.

Finnian, variation of Finn.

Flann, "red-haired," Irish Gaelic.

Fletch, short form of Fletcher.

Fletcher, originally a surname referring to an "arrow-maker," Old French.

Flint, "rock," Old English.

Florian, "flowering," Latin.

Floyd, originally a Welsh surname, a variation of Lloyd.

Flynn, "descendant of the ruddy one," Irish.

Forrest, originally a surname referring to someone from the "forest" or a "forester."

Foster, Old English surname referring to a "forester" by trade or a "foster parent."

Francesco, "Frenchman," Italian, from Latin.

Francis, English form of Francesco.

Francisco, Spanish form of Francesco.

Franco, Italian short form of Francesco.

Frank, originally a name for a Germanic people who migrated to the country later known as France. Also a short form of Francis.

Frankie, diminutive of Frank or Francis.

Franklin, originally a Middle English surname referring to a "landowner." Popularized by U.S. President Franklin D. Roosevelt.

Fraser, originally a Scottish surname, from Old French, "ash tree."

Frasier, variation of Fraser.

Frazer, variation of Fraser.

Frazier, variation of Fraser.

Fred, short form of Frederick.

Freddy, Freddie, affectionate short forms of Frederick.

Frederick, Frederic, Fredrick, from the Old German words for "peace" and "ruler."

Fritz, diminutive of Friedrich, the German form of Frederick.

Fulton, originally a Scottish surname referring to a "muddy place."

Fyfe, variation of Fife.

Fyodor, Russian form of Theodore.

Gabe, short form of Gabriel.

Gabriel, "man of God," Hebrew. In the Bible, one of the archangels.

Gahiji, "hunter," African.

Gaius, "to rejoice," Latin. Borne by the Roman emperor Gaius Julius Caesar.

Galahad, "hawk," Welsh. One of the Knights of the Round Table in Arthurian legend.

Galen, "calm," Greek.

Galway, from Irish Gaelic, "stony." A place in Ireland.

Gamal, from Arabic, "camel."

Gamaliel, "God is my reward," Hebrew.

Gareth, "gentle," from Welsh. One of the Knights of the Round Table.

Garfield, originally a surname meaning "field of spears," Old English.

Garret, Garrett, from the surnames, medieval variations of Gerard.

Garrick, originally a surname, from the Old English words for "spear" and "ruler."

Garrison, originally a surname, from Old French, "fort."

Garry, variation of Gary.

Garth, originally a surname, from Old Norse, "enclosure."

Gary, "spear," Old English.

Gaston, "from Gascony," French.

Gavin, "hawk," Celtic.

Gawain, variation of Gavin. A Knight of King Arthur's Round Table.

Gaylord, originally a surname, from Old French, "dandy."

Ged, short form of Gerard or Gerald.

Gene, short form of Eugene.

Geoff, short form of Geoffrey.

Geoffrey, from the Old German words for "peaceful" and "traveler." A popular name in the Middle Ages, borne by Chaucer, the author of *The Canterbury Tales.*

Geordie, diminutive of George.

George, from Greek, "farmer." Popularized in England by the kings and the legendary St. George, and in the U.S. by George Washington.

Georges, French form of George.

Georgie, diminutive of George.

Geraint, Welsh name, from Greek, "old."

Gerald, derived from the Old German words for "spear" and "rule."

Gerard, derived from the Old German words for "spear" and "brave."

Gerhard, Gerhart, German forms of Gerard.

Germain, French personal name, from Latin, "brother."

Gerrard, variation of Gerard.

Gerry, short form of Gerald or Gerard, or a variation of Jerry.

Gervais, French form of Gervaise.

Gervaise, Gervase, Old German, possibly from the words for "spear" and "servant."

Gibson, "son of Gilbert," English.

Gideon, "mighty warrior," Hebrew. A biblical name.

Gil, short form of Gilbert.

Gilbert, from the Old German words for "pledge" and "bright."

Giles, "young goat," Greek.

Gilroy, originally a surname meaning "servant of the red-haired man," Gaelic.

Giovanni, Italian form of John.

Giuseppe, Italian form of Joseph.

Glen, Glenn, originally a surname meaning "valley," Gaelic.

Glyn, Glynn, variations of Glenn.

Godfrey, from the Old German words for "good" and "peace." A personal name found in the Middle Ages.

Godwin, Old English personal name derived from the words for "good" and "peace."

Goldwin, Goldwyn, from an Old English personal name derived from the words for "gold" and "wine."

Gomer, "to accomplish," Hebrew. An Old Testament name.

Gonzalo, from the Old German words for "strife" and "elf."

Gordie, diminutive of Gordon.

Gordon, originally a Scottish surname referring to someone from a "great hill," Gaelic.

Gordy, diminutive of Gordon.

Grady, "noble" or "illustrious," Gaelic.

Graham, Grahame, Graeme, originally a Scottish surname referring to someone from a "gravelly homestead."

Grant, "tall, large," from Norman French. A surname in medieval times. Inspired as a first name by U.S. President Ulysses S. Grant.

Granville, "big place," Old French.

Greg, Gregg, short forms of Gregory.

Gregor, Scottish form of Gregory.

Gregory, "watchful," Greek.

Grenville, variation of Granville.

Greville, variation of Granville.

Griffin, variation of Griffith.

Griffith, English form of a Welsh name, possibly meaning "lord" or "prince."

Grover, surname referring to someone "from the grove," Old English.

Guido, Italian variation of Guy, found in the Middle Ages.

Gun, Gunn, short forms of Gunnar.

Gunnar, "battle warrior," Old Norse.

Gunther, Gunter, German forms of Gunnar.

Gus, short form of Augustus or Gustave.

Gustaf, Swedish form of Gustave.

Gustave, from Old Norse, "staff of the people."

Guthrie, "windy," Scottish.

Guy, "wide wood," Old German.

Habib, "beloved," North African.

Hadley, "meadow near the heath," Old English.

Hadrian, variation of Adrian.

Hakeem, "wise ruler," Arabic.

Hal, diminutive of Henry or Harry.

Hale, originally a surname referring to a place, Old English, or "robust, hearty," Teutonic.

Ham, "hot," Hebrew. One of Noah's sons in the Old Testament.

Hamilton, originally a Scottish surname meaning "bare hill," Old English.

Hamish, Gaelic form of James.

Hamisi, "born on Thursday," African.

Hamlet, originally a diminutive of Hamo, brought into popularity by Shakepeare's play *Hamlet*.

Hamlin, Hamlyn, variations of Hamo.

Hammond, variation of Hamo.

Hamo, "house," Old German. A common name in the Middle Ages, giving rise to a number of related surnames.

Hamon, variation of Hamo.

Hampton, "homestead," Old English.

Hank, diminutive of Henry, from medieval England.

Hannibal, found in the third century B.C., of uncertain origin.

Hans, German and Dutch form of John.

Harding, originally an Old English surname meaning "strong and brave."

Hardy, originally an Old English surname, from a nickname for a "brave man."

Harlan, originally an Old English surname referring to "rocky land."

Harley, originally an Old English surname meaning "hare wood."

Harlow, "army hill," Old English.

Harman, variation of Hermann.

Harold, Old English personal name derived from the words for "army" and "power."

Harper, "harp player," Old English.

Harris, "son of Harry," Old English.

Harrison, originally a surname meaning "son of Harry."

Harry, form of Henry in use since the Middle Ages.

Hartley, originally a surname, from the Old English words for "stag" and "clearing."

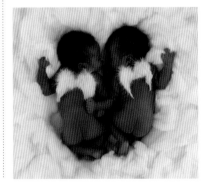

Harvey, "battle-worthy," Celtic. Originally a Breton personal name.

Haskell, "sacrificial cauldron," Old Norse. From Celtic mythology.

Hayden, originally an Old English surname referring to someone from a "hay valley."

Haydn, used as a personal name after composer Franz Joseph Haydn.

Heath, originally an Old English surname referring to someone from the "heath."

Heathcliff, "cliff with heather," Old English.

Heber, "fellowship," Hebrew.

Hector, "hold fast," Greek. In Greek legend the Trojan warrior killed by Achilles.

Hedley, originally a surname referring to a "heathery clearing," Old English.

Heinrich, German form of Henry.

Henri, French form of Henry.

Henry, from the Old German words for "home" and "ruler." Borne by eight English kings.

Herb, short form of Herbert.

Herbert, from the Old German words for "army" and "famous."

Hercules, from Greek, meaning "glory of Hera." One of the sons of Zeus.

Herman, English form of Hermann.

Hermann, Old German, "army man."

Herschel, "deer," Hebrew.

Hezekiah, "God is strength," Hebrew. An Old Testament name.

Hilaire, French form of Hilary.

Hilary, "cheerful," Latin.

Hilton, "place or farm on the hill," Old English.

Hiram, "brother of the exalted," Hebrew. The biblical King of Tyre.

Hob, diminutive of Robert, found in medieval Britain.

Holden, "deep valley," Old English.

Hollis, "holly," Old English.

Homer, "hostage," Greek.

Hooper, Old English surname for a "barrel-maker" by trade.

Hopkin, diminutive of Hob.

Horace, English form of Horatius, an Old Roman family name meaning "keeper of the hours," Latin.

Horatio, variation of Horace. Borne by British Admiral Horatio, Viscount Nelson.

Houston, "Hugh's town," Old English.

Howard, originally a surname, from the Old German words for "heart" and "protection."

Hoyt, "spirit, mind," Irish.

Hubert, Old German name meaning "heart" and "bright." The patron saint of hunters.

Hudson, "Richard's son," Old English.

Huey, diminutive of Hugh.

Hugh, "heart," Old German.

Hugo, Latinized form of Hugh.

Humbert, derived from the Old German words for "giant" and "bright."

Hume, "river island," Old Norse.

Humphrey, derived from the Old German words for "warrior" and "peace."

Hunter, originally a surname denoting a "hunter."

Hyde, "a measure of land," Old English.

Hyman, "life," Hebrew.

Hywel, Welsh personal name meaning "eminent."

Iago, Welsh, Spanish and Italian form of James. The villain in Shakespeare's *Othello*.

Iain, Gaelic form of John.

Ian, Scottish form of John.

Ichabod, "where is the glory?" Hebrew.

Idris, Welsh personal name from the words for "impulsive" and "lord."

Iggy, short form of Ignatius.

Ignace, French form of Ignatius.

Ignatius, originally an Old Roman family name, later associated with "fire," Latin.

Igor, Russian personal name, from Old Norse, "warrior."

Ike, diminutive of Isaac.

Ilya, Russian form of Elias.

Immanuel, Old Testament spelling of Emmanuel.

Ingmar, "famous son," Old Norse.

Inigo, medieval Spanish form of Ignatius.

Innes, "island," Celtic.

Ira, "watchful," Hebrew.

Irvin, Irvine, "handsome," Scottish Gaelic.

Irving, variation of Irvin.

Irwin, variation of Irvin.

Isaac, "God may smile upon me," Hebrew. In the Old Testament, the son of Abraham who was saved from being sacrificed.

Isaiah, "God's salvation," Hebrew. An Old Testament prophet.

Isiah, variation of Isaiah.

Isidore, "gift of Isis," Greek.

Israel, "God perseveres," Hebrew. The name given to Jacob and his descendants, and the name of the Jewish state.

Ivan, Russian form of John.

Ives, variation of Yves.

Ivo, German form of Yves.

Ivor, from the Old Norse words for "bow" and "army."

Jack, diminutive of Jacob or John.

Jackie, diminutive of Jack.

Jackson, from the surname meaning "son of Jack," Middle English.

Jacob, "supplanter," Hebrew. An Old Testament name.

Jacques, French form of James.

Jago, Cornish form of James.

Jaime, Spanish form of James.

Jake, diminutive of Jacob.

Jaleel, "majestic," Arabic.

Jamal, Jamaal, Jamahl, "handsome," Arabic.

James, English form of Jacob, from Hebrew, "supplanter."

Jameson, from the surname meaning "son of James."

Jamie, Scottish diminutive of James.

Jamil, variation of Jamal.

Jamison, variation of Jameson.

Jan, Dutch and Scandinavian form of John.

Janos, Hungarian form of John.

Japheth, "enlargement," Hebrew. An Old Testament name, one of Noah's sons.

Jared, "descent," Hebrew. An Old Testament name.

Jarnett, originally a surname, or a variation of Garret.

Jarred, Jarrod, variations of Jared.

Jarvis, originally a surname, the Middle English form of Gervaise.

Jason, "healer," Greek. In Greek mythology, the leader of a quest for the golden fleece.

Jasper, Jaspar, of Persian origin, "bearer of treasure." The medieval form of Caspar, one of the three wise men who bore gifts to Jesus Christ.

Javier, variation of Xavier.

Jay, from Old French, "blue jay," or a short form of any name beginning with "J."

Jayden, modern blend of Jay and Dennis.

Jean, French form of John.

Jed, originally a short form of Jedidiah.

Jedidiah, "beloved by the Lord," Hebrew. An Old Testament name.

Jeff, short form of Jeffrey or Jefferson.

Jefferson, originally a surname meaning "son of Jeffrey." Used in honor of U.S. President Thomas Jefferson.

Jeffrey, Jeffery, variations of Geoffrey.

Jem, diminutive of James or Jeremy.

Jemmy, diminutive of James, dating from medieval times.

Jenkin, surname based on the medieval personal name Jankin, a diminutive of Jan.

Jeremiah, "appointed by God," Hebrew. An Old Testament prophet.

Jeremy, English form of Jeremiah, dating from the 13th century.

Jermaine, variation of Germain.

Jerod, variation of Jared.

Jerome, "holy name," Greek.

Jeronimo, Spanish form of Jerome.

Jerry, diminutive of Jeremy.

Jervaise, variation of Gervaise.

Jess, short form of Jesse.

Jesse, "gift," Hebrew. The father of King David in the Old Testament.

Jesus, "savior," Aramaic.

Jethro, "excellence," from Hebrew. An Old Testament name.

Jim, diminutive of James.

Jimmy, Jimmie, Jimi, affectionate short forms of James.

Joachim, "established by God," Hebrew. An Old Testament name, believed to be the name of the father of the Virgin Mary.

Job, "persecuted," Hebrew. In the Old Testament, Job's faith was tested by God.

Jock, Scottish variation of Jack.

Jody, affectionate form of Jude or Joe.

Joe, short form of Joseph.

Joel, "the Lord is God," Hebrew.

Joey, diminutive of Joseph.

Joffrey, variation of Jeffrey.

Johann, German form of John.

Johannes, German form of John.

John, from Hebrew, "Jehovah has favored." Borne by John the Baptist, John the Apostle, and John the Evangelist. By the 16th century the most common boy's name.

Johnathon, variation of Jonathan.

Johnny, Johnnie, diminutives of John.

Jon, variation of John or short form of Jonathan.

Jonah, "dove," Hebrew. A prophet in the Old Testament who was swallowed by a "great fish."

Jonas, Greek, variation of Jonah found in the New Testament.

Jonathan, Jonathon, "God's gift," Hebrew. The son of King Saul whose friendship with David became a symbol of loyalty and friendship.

Jordan, "flowing down," Hebrew. After the biblical river.

Jorge, Spanish form of George.

Jose, Spanish form of Joseph.

Josef, German, Dutch and Scandinavian form of Joseph.

Joseph, "may Jehovah add (another child)." The favorite son of Jacob in the Old Testament, and the husband of the Virgin Mary.

Josh, diminutive of Joshua.

Joshua, "Jehovah is salvation," Hebrew. In the Old Testament, Moses' successor.

Josiah, "may Jehovah heal," Hebrew. One of the kings of Judah in the Old Testament.

Juan, Spanish form of John.

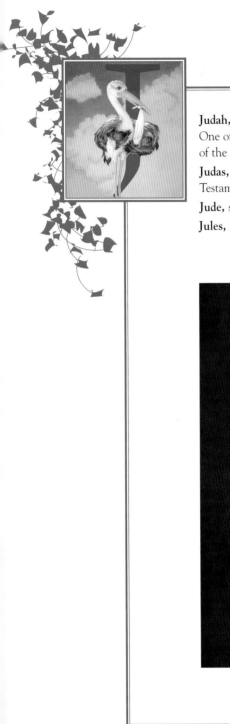

Judah, "praise," Hebrew. One of Jacob's sons and one of the twelve tribes of Israel.

Judas, Greek, New Testament form of Judah.

Jude, short form of Judas.

Jules, French form of Julius.

Julian, from the Latin personal name Julianus.

Julio, Spanish form of Julius.

Julius, originally a Roman family name, borne by Gaius Julius Caesar.

Jurgen, German form of George.

Justin, "just," Latin.

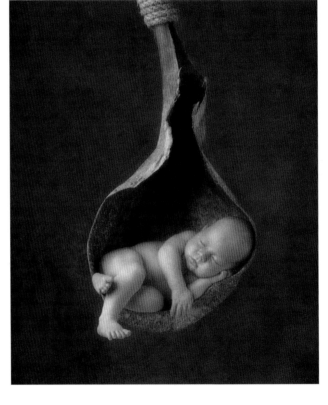

Kai, "ocean," Hawaiian, or from Welsh, "keeper of the keys."

Kain, variation of Cain.

Kalil, from Hebrew, "complete, perfect," or a variation of Khalil.

Kamal, "perfect," Arabic.

Kane, "battle," Irish Gaelic, or a variation of Cain.

Kareem, "noble," Arabic.

Karim, Karime, variations of Kareem.

Karl, German form of Charles.

Kean, Keane, English forms of Cian.

Keanu, from a Hawaiian personal name meaning "breeze."

Keefe, originally an Irish surname meaning "kind, gentle."

Keegan, originally a surname, a form of Cian.

Keenan, from the Irish Gaelic words for "little" and "ancient."

Keifer, variation of Kiefer.

Keir, Scottish surname, a variation of Kerr.

Keiran, variation of Kieran.

Keith, originally a Scottish surname derived from the Celtic word for "wood."

Kelan, "slender," Irish Gaelic.

Kelly, from a traditional Irish Gaelic personal name, possibly meaning "church."

Kelsey, Old English surname derived from the words for "ship" and "victory."

Kelvin, modern coinage referring to the Scottish river.

Kemp, originally a surname meaning "athlete" or "warrior," Old English.

Ken, originally a short form of Kenneth.

Kendall, Kendal, "chief of the valley," Celtic.

Kendrick, originally a surname, possibly from Welsh origins, "son of Henry."

Kenelm, derived from the Old English words for "brave" and "helmet."

Kennedy, from an Irish Gaelic traditional name derived from the words for "head" and "ugly." Associated with the U.S. political family.

Kenneth, from Scottish Gaelic, "handsome," or from Irish Gaelic, "fire-born."

Kenny, diminutive of Kenneth.

Kenrick, variation of Kendrick.

Kent, originally a surname derived from the English county, possibly from Celtic, "coast."

Kentigern, "chief lord," Celtic.

Kerr, originally a surname referring to someone who lived by a "patch of wet ground overgrown with brushwood," Old Norse.

Kerry, "descendants of Ciar," Irish Gaelic. From the Irish county.

Kevin, "handsome," Irish Gaelic.

Khahil, variation of Khalil.

Khalil, "good friend," Arabic.

Kiefer, "barrel-maker," from German.

Kieran, English form of Ciaran.

Killian, "strife," Irish Gaelic.

Kim, diminutive of Kimball or Kimberley.

Kimball, originally a surname, possibly derived from the Old English words for "family" and "bold."

King, the title of a monarch, also a surname for royal staff.

Kingsley, originally a surname referring to the "king's meadow," Old English.

Kip, affectionate short form of Christopher.

Kirby, from Old Norse, originally a surname referring to the "church farm."

Kirk, originally a surname, from Old Norse, "church."

Kit, affectionate short form of Christopher.

Knut, from Old Norse, "knot." Originally a nickname for a Viking, referring to a short, squat appearance.

Konrad, German variation of Conrad.

Koren, "shining," Hebrew.

Kris, Scandinavian short form of Kristofer.

Krishna, "dark," Hindi. An incarnation of Vishnu.

Kristian, variation of Christian.

Kristofer, Kristopher, Scandinavian forms of Christopher.

Kumar, "youth," Hindi.

Kurt, diminutive of Konrad.

Kwame, Kwami, "born on Saturday," African.

Kyle, "narrow," Gaelic. Originally a Scottish surname.

Kyran, variation of Kieran.

Laban, "white," Hebrew. From the Old Testament.

Lachlan, from Scottish Gaelic, referring to someone from Norway, "land of fiords."

Lafayette, "beech tree grove," a French place name and family name. Used as a personal name in honor of the aide to George Washington.

Laird, "landowner," Celtic.

Lamar, "famous throughout the land," Teutonic.

Lambert, originally a surname of Germanic origin, derived from the words for "land" and "famous."

Lamont, "law man," Old Norse.

Lance, from Old German, "land," or from Latin, "light spear."

Lancelot, diminutive of Lance. The famous Knight of the Round Table in Arthurian legends.

Landon, originally a surname, from Old English, "long hill."

Lane, surname referring to someone who lives near a "lane or path."

Larry, Larrie, short forms of Laurence.

Lars, Scandinavian form of Laurence.

Lateef, "pleasant, gentle," North African.

Laurence, French, from a Latin name meaning "man from Laurentum."

Laurie, affectionate short form of Laurence.

Lawrence, variation of Laurence.

Leander, from Greek, "lion" and "man."
In Greek mythology, the lover of Hero.

Lee, Old English surname meaning "from the wood."

Leif, "beloved," Old Norse.

Leigh, variation of Lee.

Leighton, originally a surname, "herb garden," Old English.

Leith, from Scottish Gaelic, "wet."

Leland, originally a surname for someone living on "fallow land."

Lemuel, "devoted to God," Hebrew. The hero of *Gulliver's Travels*.

Len, short form of Leonard.

Lennan, from Irish Gaelic, "darling." A personal name dating from medieval times.

Lennard, variation of Leonard.

Lennox, originally a Scottish surname, the name of an earldom.

Leo, "lion," Latin.

Leon, variation of Leo.

Leonard, from the Old German words for "lion" and "brave."

Leonardo, Italian and Spanish form of Leonard.

Leopold, from the Old German words for "people" and "bold."

Leroy, "the king," Old French.

Les, short form of Leslie.

Leslie, Lesley, originally a Scottish surname, possibly from Gaelic, "court of hollies." Leslie is the usual masculine spelling.

Lester, originally a surname referring to the English town of Leicester.

Levi, "attached, pledged," Hebrew. In the Old Testament, one of the sons of Jacob and Leah.

Levon, variation of Levi.

Levy, variation of Levi.

Lewis, English form of Louis.

Lex, short form of Alexander.

Liam, Irish Gaelic short form of William.

Lincoln, originally a surname referring to Lincoln in England. Given in honor of U.S. President Abraham Lincoln.

Linden, Lindon, variations of Lyndon.

Lindsay, Lindsey, originally a Scottish surname, from a place name.

Linford, originally a surname meaning "from the lime tree ford," Old English.

Linus, "flaxen-haired," Greek. The musician who taught Hercules.

Lionel, medieval diminutive of Leo.

Llewelyn, Welsh, possibly derived from the words for "leader" or "lion."

Lloyd, Welsh surname meaning "gray."

Lockwood, "enclosed wood," Old English.

Logan, Scottish surname, from a place name meaning "little hollow."

Lorenzo, Spanish and Italian form of Laurence.

Lorne, Lorn, originally the name of a Scottish chieftain, then a place name.

Lothair, from the Old German words for "fame" and "army."

Lothar, variation of Lothair.

Lou, short form of Louis.

Louis, French name of Old German origin, meaning "famous warrior." A name found in French nobility.

Lovell, originally a surname, from an Old French nickname, "wolf cub."

Lowell, "the beloved one," Old English. A surname of a prominent U.S. family.

Loyd, variation of Lloyd.

Lucas, Latin form of Luke, common in medieval times and surviving as a surname.

Lucian, variation of Lucien.

Luciano, Italian and Spanish form of Lucien.

Lucien, from a Latin name meaning "bringing light."

Lucius, from Latin, "light."

Ludwig, German form of Louis.

Luigi, Italian form of Louis.

Luis, Spanish form of Louis.

Luke, from a Greek name meaning "of Luciana." The patron saint of doctors and artists.

Luther, from a German surname derived from the words for "people" and "army."

Lyle, from French, "the island." Originally a surname.

Lyman, "from the pasture," Old English.

Lyndon, "hill of linden trees," Old English.

Lynn, "stream," Old English. Originally a place name and family name.

Mac, Mack, "son of," Scottish. Often a nickname or short form of names beginning "Mac."

Macauley, "son of Amalgaid," originally a Scottish or Irish surname.

Mace, variation of Mason.

Mackenzie, originally a Scottish surname meaning "handsome."

Maclean, "son of Leander," Scottish Gaelic.

Madison, Maddison, "son of Maud," from Middle English.

Madoc, "fortunate," a traditional Welsh personal name.

Magnus, "great," Latin. Borne by a number of Scandinavian kings in medieval times.

Mahlon, "rare," Hebrew. From the Old Testament.

Malachy, Irish form of the Hebrew name Malachi, meaning "my messenger."

Malcolm, "servant of Columba," from Gaelic.

Mallory, "unhappy" or "unfortunate," originally a surname derived from French.

Malon, variation of Mahlon.

Manasseh, "forget," Hebrew. From the Old Testament.

Manfred, derived from the Old German words for "man" and "people."

Manley, originally a surname derived from the vocabulary word "manly."

Mansel, Mansell, derived from a surname, possibly from the French place name Le Mans.

Manuel, Spanish form of Emmanuel.

Maoz, "strength," Hebrew.

Marc, French form of Mark.

Marcel, French form of Marcellus.

Marcellus, originally a Roman family name, from Mars, the Roman god of war.

Marco, Italian form of Mark.

Marcos, Spanish form of Mark.

Marcus, original Latin form of Mark.

Marek, variation of Mark.

Mario, Italian form of Mark.

Mark, English form of the Latin name Marcus, possibly from Mars, the Roman god of war.

Marlon, of uncertain origin, possibly a diminutive of Marc, or a variation of Merlin.

Marmaduke, from an Old Irish name meaning "servant of Maedoc."

Marquis, "count of a borderland," from Latin. A title of nobility in England and France.

Marrin, Marryn, medieval variations of Merfyn.

Marsh, short form of Marshall.

Marshall, originally a surname, from Old French, "horse servant."

Martin, from Latin, after Mars, the Roman god of war.

Marton, variation of Martin.

Marty, diminutive of Martin.

Martyn, variation of Martin.

Marvin, Marven, medieval variations of Merfyn.

Mason, originally a surname referring to a "stoneworker" by trade, Old French.

Mathew, variation of Matthew.

Mathias, variation of Matthias.

Matt, diminutive of Matthew.

Matthew, "gift of the Lord," Hebrew. The writer of the first gospel in the New Testament.

Matthias, Greek form of Matthew.

Matty, Mattie, affectionate short forms of Matthew.

Maurice, from Latin, "dark, swarthy."

Max, short form of Maximilian or Maxwell.

Maximilian, "the greatest," Latin, dating from the third century.

Maxwell, Scottish surname meaning "Magnus' well".

Maynard, originally a surname, from Old German, "strength."

Mel, short form of Melvin.

Melvin, Melvyn, of uncertain origin, possibly from Irish Gaelic, "gentle chief."

Merce, variation of Mercer.

Mercer, "merchant," Old English.

Meredith, "great lord," Old Welsh.

Merfyn, traditional Welsh personal name, possibly meaning "famous friend."

Merlin, from the Old Celtic words for "sea" and "hill, fort." In Arthurian legends, the wizard who advised King Arthur and his father.

Merrill, from Gaelic, "sea-bright."

Mervyn, Mervin, English forms of Merfyn.

Micah, variation of Michael found in the Old Testament.

Michael, "who is like Jehovah," Hebrew. One of the archangels in the Bible.

Michel, French form of Michael.

Mick, diminutive of Michael.

Mickey, Micky, diminutives of Michael.

Miguel, Spanish form of Michael.

Mike, short form of Michael.

Mikhail, Russian form of Michael.

Miles, possibly a variation of Michael or Milo, or from Latin, "soldier."

Milo, Latinized form of Miles found in the Middle Ages.

Milos, variation of Milo.

Milton, originally a surname meaning "from the mill town," Old English. First used as a personal name in honor of English poet John Milton.

Mitch, short form of Mitchell.

Mitchell, originally a surname derived from the medieval form of Michael.

Mo, Moe, diminutives of Moses.

Mohammed, "praised," Arabic. The founder of the Islamic religion.

Monroe, originally a Scottish surname referring to the River Roe, Ireland.

Montague, Norman surname referring to Montaigu, France.

Monte, diminutive of Montague or Montgomery.

Montgomery, originally a Norman surname meaning "Gumric's hill," Gumric being a "powerful man."

Monty, diminutive of Montague or Montgomery.

Moray, variation of Murray.

Mordecai, "belonging to Marduk," Hebrew.

Morgan, traditional boy's name in Wales, from Old Welsh, "circle."

Morley, originally a surname referring to someone from the "marsh meadow," Old English.

Morris, variation of Maurice.

Morrison, "son of Maurice," Old English.

Mort, short form of Mortimer or Morton.

Mortimer, originally a surname, from a Norman French place name meaning "still water."

Morton, originally a surname referring to someone from a "marshy farm," Old English.

Moses, possibly Hebrew or Egyptian, "son." In the Old Testament, God's chosen one who led the Israelites to the promised land.

Moshe, Hebrew form of Moses.

Moss, variation of Moses dating to the Middle Ages.

Mozes, variation of Moses.

Muhammed, Muhammad, variations of Mohammed.

Muir, Scottish surname meaning "moor."

Mungo, Scottish, possibly meaning "friend" or "beloved."

Munro, Munroe, variations of Monroe.

Murray, Scottish surname meaning "sea."

Myles, variation of Miles.

Myron, "myrrh," Greek.

Nahum, "comforting," Hebrew. An Old Testament name.

Napoleon, of uncertain origin, possibly meaning "from Naples." Given as a personal name to honor Napoleon Bonaparte.

Natan, variation of Nathan.

Nathan, "gift," Hebrew. A prophet in the Old Testament.

Nathaniel, "gift," Hebrew.

Neal, Neale, variations of Neil.

Ned, short form of Edward or Edwin.

Nehemiah, "consolation of the Lord," Hebrew.

Neil, Scottish form of Niall.

Neill, variation of Neil.

Nelson, originally a surname meaning "son of Neil," Old English.

Nevada, "snowy," Spanish. Also a place name.

Neville, originally a surname referring to the "new town," French.

Nevin, "nephew," Gaelic.

Niall, Irish Gaelic, possibly "champion" or "leader."

Nicholas, from the Greek words for "victory" and "people." A fourth-century saint, and patron saint of Greece, of Russia and of children.

Nick, short form of Nicholas.

Nicky, affectionate short form of Nicholas.

Nicol, Scottish form of Nicholas.

Nicolas, Spanish form of Nicholas.

Niels, Danish form of Nicholas.

Nigel, Latinized form of Neil, or from Latin, "black."

Nikolai, Russian form of Nicholas.

Niles, variation of Nicholas.

Ninian, of uncertain origin, the name of a fifth-century saint.

Noah, "long-lived," Hebrew.

Noam, "pleasant," Hebrew.

Noel, "Christmas," Old French.

Nolan, originally an Irish Gaelic surname meaning "chariot-fighter."

Norbert, from the Old German words for "north" and "bright."

Norm, short form of Norman.

Norman, from German, "man of the north."

Norris, originally a Norman surname, "person from the north."

Norton, originally a surname referring to the "town of the north."

Nouri, popular Persian name meaning "prince" or "light."

Nowell, variation of Noel.

Obadiah, "servant of God," Hebrew. A prophet in the Old Testament.

Oberon, variation of Auberon. The king of the fairies in *A Midsummer Night's Dream*.

Octavius, originally a Roman family name, from Latin, "eighth."

Odo, "wealth, prosperity," Old German.

Ogden, surname referring to the "oak valley," Old English.

Ogilvie, Ogilvy, from Welsh, "high."

Olaf, from the Old Norse words for "ancestor" and "relics." The patron saint of Norway.

Olav, Danish form of Olaf.

Oliver, English form of Olivier.

Olivier, French personal name. From Latin, "olive tree."

Oman, "eloquent," Hebrew, or from Arabic, "thriving."

Omar, "long life," Arabic.

Oran, from Irish Gaelic, "sallow."

Oren, "tree," Hebrew.

Orien, variation of Orion.

Orion, "son of light," Greek. A famed hunter in Greek mythology.

Orlando, Italian form of Roland. The hero of Shakespeare's play *As You Like It*.

Orsino, Italian form of Orson.

Orson, surname derived from a Norman French nickname, "bear cub."

Orville, coined in the 18th century for a novel, from Old French, "from the golden place."

Osbert, from the Old English words for "god" and "bright."

Osborn, Osborne, derived from the Old English words for "god" and "bear, warrior."

Oscar, from the Irish Gaelic words for "deer" and "friend," or from Old English, "god" and "spear."

Osmond, from the Old English words for "god" and "protector."

Ossian, an Irish Gaelic personal name of uncertain origin.

Ossy, Ossie, affectionate short forms of Oscar and Oswald.

Oswald, from the Old English words for "god" and "power."

Oswin, from the Old English words for "god" and "friend."

Otis, originally a surname derived from Odo.

Otto, German form of Odo.

Owain, Old Welsh form of Euan.

Owen, modern Welsh form of Euan.

Pablo, Spanish form of Paul.

Paddy, diminutive of Patrick.

Padraig, Irish Gaelic form of Patrick.

Paine, "countryman," Old French.

Palmer, originally a surname meaning "pilgrim," Old French.

Pancho, Spanish diminutive of Francisco.

Paolo, Italian form of Paul.

Paris, "from Paris," Gaulish, or after the character in Greek mythology who eloped with Helen of Troy.

Parker, "park-keeper," Old English.

Parnell, short form of Petronel, originally a surname.

Parrish, surname meaning "from Paris."

Parry, originally a surname meaning "son of Harry," Welsh.

Pascal, "of Easter," French, from Latin.

Pascoe, variation of Pascal.

Pat, short form of Patrick.

Paton, diminutive of Patrick.

Patrice, French form of Patrick.

Patrick, "nobleman," from Latin. The patron saint of Ireland.

Patton, diminutive of Patrick.

Paul, "small," originally a Roman family name. St. Paul was a founder of the Christian church.

Payton, Scottish form of Patrick.

Pearce, originally a surname derived from the personal name Piers.

Pedro, Spanish form of Peter.

Percival, possibly from Old French, "pierce" and "valley." A Knight of King Arthur's Round Table.

Percy, originally an aristocratic surname from a Norman village, popularized by poet Percy Bysshe Shelley. Also a short form of Percival.

Peregrine, "foreigner," from Latin.

Pernell, variation of Parnell.

Perry, short form of Peregrine, or from the Old English surname meaning "pear tree."

Perse, variation of Piers.

Pete, short form of Peter.

Peter, from Greek, "stone." The name given to Jesus' disciple Simon.

Peyton, from the place name meaning "Paega's farm," Old English.

Phil, short form of Philip.

Philip, "lover of horses," a Greek personal name from classical times.

Philippe, French form of Philip.

Phillip, variation of Philip.

Philo, "friendly," Greek.

Phineas, Old Testament name meaning "oracle," Hebrew.

Piaras, Irish Gaelic form of Piers dating from the Middle Ages.

Pierce, variation of Piers.

Pierre, French form of Peter.

Piers, Middle English form of Peter.

Pius, "dutiful," Latin.

Placido, "untroubled, faithful," from Latin.

Plato, "broad-shouldered," Greek. The student of Socrates and teacher of Aristotle.

Porter, originally a surname, "door-keeper," from Old French.

Powell, "son of Howell," Welsh.

Prescott, originally a surname, from the Old English words for "priest" and "dwelling."

Preston, originally a surname referring to the "priest's town," Old English.

Primo, "first," Latin.

Prince, "first place," from Latin. A royal title.

Purvis, "provider," Latin. An occupational name.

Quentin, Quenten, "fifth," Latin.
Quincy, variation of Quentin.
Quinn, short form of Quentin.

Quintin, Quinton, variations of Quentin.
Quito, Ecuador, a place name.

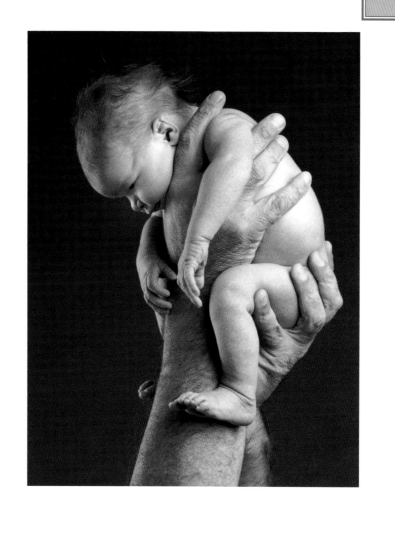

Rabbie, Scottish diminutive of Robert.

Rafael, Spanish form of Raphael.

Rainer, German form of Rayner.

Rainier, French form of Rayner.

Raja, "king, ruler," Hindi.

Raji, variation of Raja.

Rajir, variation of Raja.

Ralph, Ralf, from the Old German words for "counsel" and "wolf."

Ramon, Spanish form of Raymond.

Ramsay, Ramsey, originally a surname, from a place name meaning "garlic" and "island."

Ranald, Scottish form of Reginald or Ronald.

Rand, short form of Randall.

Randall, Randell, common forms of Randolph dating from medieval times. From the Old English words for "shield rim."

Randolph, Randolf, personal names dating from the Middle Ages. From the Old English words for "shield rim" and "wolf."

Randy, short form of Randall or Randolph.

Ranulph, Ranulf, Scottish personal name, from the Old Norse words for "advice" and "wolf."

Raoul, French form of Ralph.

Raphael, "God has healed," Hebrew.

Rashad, "spiritual guidance," Arabic.

Rasheed, "mature," Arabic.

Rasmu, short form of Erasmus.

Rastus, short form of Erastus, "to love," Greek.

Raven, from Old English, the name of the bird.

Ray, short form of Raymond, or from French, "king."

Raymond, derived from the Old German words for "advice" and "protector."

Raymund, variation of Raymond.

Rayner, Raynor, originally a surname, from the Old German words for "counsel" and "army."

Read, Reade, originally a surname, from an Old English nickname for a "red-haired person."

Red, affectionate name for a "red-haired person."

Redmond, from an Irish Gaelic form of Raymond.

Reece, variation of Rhys.

Reg, short form of Reginald.

Reggie, diminutive of Reginald.

Reginald, Latinized form of Reynold.

Regis, "ruler," Old Provençal.

Reid, originally a surname derived from an Old English nickname for a "red-haired person."

Reinaldo, Spanish form of Reynold.

Reinhold, German form of Reynold.

Remington, originally a surname referring to someone from the "town by the stream," Old English.

Renald, variation of Reynold.

Renaldo, variation of Reinaldo.

Rene, French, "born again," from Latin Renatus.

Reuben, "behold a son," Hebrew. In the Old Testament, Jacob's eldest son.

Reuven, variation of Reuben.

Rex, "king," Latin.

Reynard, from the Old German words for "counsel" and "hard," or from Old French, "fox."

Reynaud, French form of Reynold.

Reynold, Norman personal name, from the Old German words for "advice" and "ruler."

Rhett, originally a surname, popularized as a personal name after the novel and film *Gone with the Wind*.

Rhodri, Old Welsh, from the words for "wheel" and "ruler."

Rhys, "ardor," a traditional Welsh personal name.

Ricardo, Spanish form of Richard.

Rich, short form of Richard.

Richard, "strong ruler," an Old French personal name of Germanic origin. Borne by Richard the Lionheart of England.

Richie, diminutive of Richard.

Richmond, "splendid hill," Old French.

Rick, diminutive of Richard.

Ricky, Rickie, diminutives of Richard.

Rico, variation of Richard.

Ridley, originally a surname based on a place name meaning "burnt field."

Rigby, "ridge farm," Old Norse.

Riley, originally a surname referring to someone from a "rye field."

Rinaldo, Italian variation of Reynold.

Ringo, modern coinage popularized by Beatle Ringo Starr.

Rip, "ripe, full grown," Dutch.

Ritchie, diminutive of Richard.

Roald, Scandinavian personal name, from the Old Norse words for "fame" and "ruler."

Rob, short form of Robert or Robin.

Robbie, diminutive of Robert or Robin.

Robert, French personal name derived from the Old German words for "fame" and "bright." Borne by Robert the Bruce of Scotland, who freed the Scots from British rule.

Roberto, Spanish and Italian form of Robert.

Robin, originally a diminutive of Robert.

Robinson, "son of Robin."

Rocco, Italian personal name, from Old German, "rest." Also an affectionate form of Richard.

Rock, from the vocabulary word, possibly because of its associations with "stability" and "reliability."

Rockwell, originally a surname referring to someone from a "rocky stream."

Rocky, variation of Rocco.

Rod, short form of Roderick or Rodney.

Roderick, Roderic, from the Old German words for "fame" and "rule."

Rodger, variation of Roger.

Rodney, originally a surname referring to the "cleared land near the water," Old English.

Rodolf, German and Dutch form of Rudolf.

Rodolfo, Italian and Spanish form of Rudolf.

Rodolphe, French form of Rudolf.

Rodrick, variation of Roderick.

Rodrigo, Spanish form of Roderick.

Roger, Old French personal name, from the Old German words for "fame" and "spear."

Rogers, "son of Roger," Middle English.

Roland, "famous in the land," Old German.

Rolf, "famous wolf," Old German.

Rollo, variation of Rolf dating from the Middle Ages.

Rolph, variation of Rolf.

Roly, diminutive of Roland.

Romain, French form of Roman.

Roman, "from Rome," from the Latin personal name Romanus.

Romano, Italian form of Roman.

Romanos, variation of Roman.

Romeo, "pilgrim to Rome," Latin. Immortalized as the tragic lover in Shakespeare's *Romeo and Juliet.*

Ron, short form of Ronald.

Ronald, from an Old Norse personal name meaning "power."

Ronan, "seal," Irish Gaelic.

Ronny, Ronnie, diminutives of Ronald.

Rory, from Irish Gaelic, "red-haired king."

Roscoe, originally a surname, from the Old Norse words for "deer" and "wood."

Ross, originally a Scottish surname meaning "moorland."

Rowan, "little red one," Irish Gaelic.

Rowland, variation of Roland.

Roy, from Gaelic, "red," a Scottish personal name, or from Old French, "king."

Royce, from the Old German words for "fame" and "type."

Royden, "rye hill," Old English.

Royston, originally a surname referring to an Old English place name meaning "by a stone cross."

Ruben, variation of Reuben.

Rudolf, Rudolph, "famous wolf," from Old German. A hereditary name of the Austrian nobility.

Rudy, affectionate short form of Rudolf.

Rufus, "man with red hair," Latin.

Rupert, variation of Robert.

Russell, Russel, originally a surname, from Old French, "one with red hair."

Rusty, affectionate short form of Russell, a nickname for a "red-haired person."

Rutger, Dutch form of Roger.

Rutherford, originally a surname, "cattle ford," Old English.

Ryan, from Irish Gaelic, "little king."

Sabin, "Sabine man," after the ancient tribe from near Rome.

Sacha, French diminutive of Alexander.

Sacheverell, surname of uncertain origin, possibly from French, "without kid gloves."

Salamon, variation of Solomon.

Salvador, "savior," Spanish, from Latin.

Salvatore, Italian form of Salvador.

Sam, short form of Samuel or Samson.

Sammy, Sammie, affectionate short forms of Samuel or Samson.

Samson, "sun child," Hebrew. In the Old Testament, Samson was famous for his strength.

Samuel, "name of God," Hebrew. The Old Testament prophet who anointed Saul and David as the first kings of Israel.

Sandy, diminutive of Alexander.

Sargent, "server," Latin.

Sasha, Russian diminutive of Alexander.

Saul, "prayed for," Hebrew. The name of one of the first kings of Israel.

Sawyer, "sawer of wood," Old English.

Schuyler, "teacher," Dutch. Given in honor of U.S. soldier and statesman Philip John Schuyler.

Scott, "Scotsman," Old English.

Scotty, Scottie, affectionate forms of Scott.

Seamas, Seamus, Irish Gaelic forms of James.

Sean, Irish Gaelic form of John.

Seb, short form of Sebastian.

Sebastian, from Latin, "man from Sebastia," dating from the third century.

Selby, originally a surname, possibly from the Old English words for "prosperity" and "friend," or from Latin, "wood."

Selwyn, originally a surname, "of the woods," Latin.

Septimus, "seventh," Latin.

Serge, French form of Sergius.

Sergio, Italian form of Sergius.

Sergius, Latin name of uncertain origin, possibly meaning "servant."

Seth, "appointed," Hebrew. In the Old Testament, the third son of Adam and Eve.

Sextus, "sixth," Latin.

Seymour, originally an aristocratic surname, from the French place name St. Maur.

Shane, English variation of Sean.

Shaun, Shawn, variations of Sean.

Sheldon, originally a surname referring to someone from a "slightly sloping hill," Old English.

Sheridan, "wild man," Celtic.

Sherlock, "bright, fair hair," Old English.

Sherman, "sheep shearer," Old English.

Shimon, "astonished, amazed," Hebrew.

Sid, short form of Sidney.

Sidney, originally a surname referring to St. Denis in France, or from Old English, "wide meadow."

Siegfried, Siegfrid, "victorious peace," Old German.

Sigmund, from the Old German words for "victory" and "protection."

Silas, variation of Latin Silvanus dating from the first century, meaning "of the trees."

Silvester, "of the woods," Latin.

Simeon, "hearkening," Hebrew.

Simon, English form of Simeon.

Sinclair, originally a Scottish surname, from the French town St. Clair.

Skip, "shipmaster," Old Norse.

Skyler, Skylar, variations of Schuyler.

Sly, diminutive of Sylvester.

Solomon, "peace," Hebrew. In the Old Testament, the wise King of Israel.

Spencer, Spenser, originally a surname for a steward, Middle English.

Stacy, Stacey, diminutives of Eustace.

Stan, short form of Stanley.

Stanley, originally a surname referring to a "rocky meadow," Old English.

Stanly, variation of Stanley.

Stefan, Scandinavian, German and Russian form of Stephen.

Stephan, German form of Stephen.

Stephen, "crown," Greek. The first Christian martyr.

Sterling, originally a surname, possibly from Old English, "starling" or "little star."

Steve, short form of Stephen.

Steven, variation of Stephen.

Stevie, diminutive of Stephen.

Stewart, variation of Stuart.

Stirling, variation of Sterling.

Strom, "stream," German.

Stuart, originally a Scottish surname, from Old English, "steward." The ruling house of Scotland from the 14th to the 18th century.

Sydney, variation of Sidney, also a place name.

Sylvester, variation of Silvester.

Tad, diminutive of Thaddeus.

Talbot, originally an aristocratic surname, Old English.

Tam, Scottish diminutive of Thomas.

Tanner, originally a surname, from Old English, referring to a "tanner" by trade.

Tarquin, of uncertain origin. Borne by kings of Rome, B.C.

Taylor, originally a surname referring to a "tailor," Old English.

Tecumseh, Native American, after a famous Shawnee chief.

Ted, diminutive of Edward, Edwin or Edmund.

Teddy, Teddie, affectionate short forms of Edward, Edwin or Edmund.

Terence, originally a Roman family name, possibly derived from the name of a goddess associated with the harvest.

Terrance, variation of Terence.

Terrell, originally a surname, possibly related to Tyrell.

Terrence, variation of Terence.

Terry, medieval personal name derived from the Old German words for "race" and "power." Also a diminutive of Terence.

Tex, from the nickname for a Texan.

Thad, Thadde, short forms of Thaddeus.

Thaddeus, "valiant," Hebrew.

Thaine, variation of Thane.

Thane, "warrior," Old English.

Thayne, variation of Thane.

Theo, short form of Theodore or Theobald.

Theobald, Old German personal name, from the words for "people" and "brave."

Theodore, French form of a Greek personal name, from the words for "god" and "gift."

Theodoros, original Greek form of Theodore.

Thomas, "twin," Aramaic. In the New Testament, the apostle who would not believe in the resurrection until he had touched Christ's wounds.

Tim, short form of Timothy.

Timmy, Timmie, diminutives of Timothy.

Timothy, Greek personal name meaning "honor god."

Tito, Italian and Spanish form of Titus.

Titus, of uncertain meaning, a Roman personal name dating from the first century.

Tobias, biblical name meaning "the Lord is good," Hebrew.

Toby, affectionate short form of Tobias.

Todd, originally a surname derived from a nickname meaning "fox," Celtic.

Tom, short form of Thomas.

Tomas, Gaelic form of Thomas.

Tommy, Tommie, diminutives of Thomas.

Tonio, Italian short form of Antonio.

Tony, short form of Anthony.

Torquil, traditional Gaelic name, from the Old Norse words for "Thor" and "helmet."

Tracy, Tracey, originally a surname, from the Roman personal name Thracius.

Travis, originally a surname, "toll collector," Middle English.

Trent, originally a surname referring to the English river and place name.

Trenton, from the name of the city in New Jersey, site of an important American victory in the War of Independence.

Trevor, originally a surname, from Welsh, "large village."

Tristan, Tristin, variations of Tristram.

Tristram, from a Celtic personal name meaning "loud noise" or "sad."

Troy, originally a surname referring to the town of Troyes in France, Middle English.

Truman, "loyal man," Old English.

Tucker, "to torment," from Old English. Through Middle English, an occupational name meaning "to stretch cloth."

Tudur, traditional Welsh name derived from the Celtic words for "people" and "king."

Turlough, Irish Gaelic form of Terence.

Ty, short form of names beginning "Ty-."

Tyler, originally a surname meaning "tile-maker," Old English.

Tyrell, "stubborn person," Old French.

Tyrone, from the name of the Irish county.

Tyson, originally a surname, from either the medieval female personal name Dye, or from Old French, "firebrand."

Ulric, from the Old German words for "wolf" and "ruler."

Ultan, Irish nickname for an Ulsterman.

Ulysses, Latin form of the Greek Odysseus, of uncertain origin, possibly meaning "to hate."

Upton, "upper town," Old English.

Urbain, variation of Urban.

Urban, "city-dweller," Latin.

Uri, "light," Hebrew.

Uriah, "God is light," Hebrew. An Old Testament name.

Uriel, from Hebrew, "light" and "God." From the Old Testament genealogies.

Urien, Welsh personal name, from Celtic, "privileged birth."

Urvan, Russian form of Urban.

Val, short form of Valentine.

Valentine, "strong, healthy," Latin. A Roman martyr of the third century who gave his name to the festival of love and romance.

Valentino, Italian form of Valentine.

Valerian, "healthy," Latin.

Valerio, Italian form of Valerian.

Van, short form of Evan, Ivan, Vance or Vanya.

Vance, "marshes," Old English.

Vanya, Russian diminutive of Ivan.

Varick, "sea drifter," Icelandic.

Varrick, variation of Warwick.

Vasili, Russian form of Basil.

Vaughan, Vaughn, "small," Welsh. A nickname which became a surname.

Vergil, variation of Virgil.

Vern, Verne, short forms of Vernon.

Vernon, "alder tree," Old French.

Vic, short form of Victor.

Victor, "conqueror," Latin.

Viktor, German and Scandinavian form of Victor.

Vince, short form of Vincent.

Vincent, Old French form of a Latin name meaning "conquering."

Vincenzo, Italian form of Vincent.

Vinny, Vinnie, affectionate short forms of Vincent or Melvyn.

Virgil, from Latin, "strong, flourishing." First used as a personal name to honor the Roman poet.

Vishnu, "to pervade," Sanskrit. Second god of the Hindu trinity.

Vito, "life," Latin.

Vittorio, Italian form of Victor.

Vivian, "alive," Latin.

Vlad, variation of Vladas.

Vladas, "ruling," Slavonic.

Vladimir, "ruling power," Slavonic.

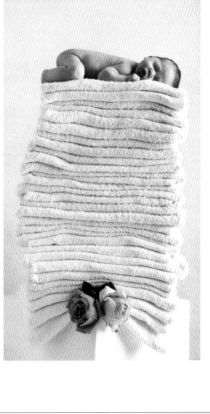

Wade, originally a surname, "to go," Old English.

Waine, variation of Wayne.

Walden, "woods," Old English.

Waldo, short form of an Old German personal name meaning "ruler."

Walker, originally a surname, referring to the trade of "one who cleans and thickens cloth," Old English.

Wallace, "foreigner," Norman French.

Wally, Wallie, diminutives of Wallace or Walter.

Walt, short form of Walter.

Walter, from the Old German words for "rule" and "folk."

Ward, originally a surname referring to a "watchman" by trade, Old English.

Warner, surname derived from the Old German words for "guard" and "army."

Warren, originally a surname referring to a "game park." Also from a personal name derived from Old German, "guard."

Warrick, variation of Warwick.

Warwick, originally a surname referring to a "dairy farm at the weir," Old English.

Washington, "settlement of Wassa's people," Old English. First used as a personal name in honor of U.S. President George Washington.

Watkin, affectionate form of Walter dating from medieval times.

Wayland, from the Old German words for "war" and "territory."

Waylon, variation of Wayland.

Wayne, derived from the Old English word for "wagon," a nickname for a "cart-driver."

Webb, originally a surname referring to a "weaver" by trade, Old English.

Webster, variation of Webb.

Welby, "farm," Old English.

Weldon, "hill by the well," Old English.

Wendell, Old German ethnic name for a Slavic people in eastern Germany.

Wentworth, "winter hut," Old English.

Werner, German, Dutch and Scandinavian form of Warner.

Wes, short form of Wesley.

Wesley, "west meadow," Old English. Used in honor of John Wesley, who founded the Methodist church.

Weston, "west farm," Old English.

Wilbur, originally a surname, from the Old English words for "will" and "fortress."

Wiley, "difficult stream," Old English.

Wilfred, Wilfrid, Wilfried, from an Old English personal name derived from the words for "will" and "peace."

Will, short form of William.

Willard, originally a surname derived from an Old English personal name meaning "will" and "brave."

Willem, Dutch form of William.

William, derived from the Old German words for "will" and "protect." Introduced to Britain by William the Conquerer in the 11th century.

Willy, Willie, diminutives of William.

Wilmer, Old English personal name derived from the words for "will" and "famous."

Wilmot, medieval diminutive of William.

Wilson, "son of William," Old English.

Winn, variation of Wynn.

Winston, originally a surname, from the Old English words for "joy" and "stone." First found in the Churchill family of England.

Winthrop, surname referring to "Wynna's farm," Old English.

Winton, Old English surname meaning "pasture" or "willow."

Wolfgang, "advancing wolf," Old German.

Wood, short form of names such as Elwood.

Woodie, short form of names such as Woodrow.

Woodrow, originally a surname referring to someone from a "row of cottages." Popularized by U.S. President Woodrow Wilson.

Woody, short form of names such as Woodrow.

Wyatt, originally a surname derived from a medieval personal name meaning "war" and "brave."

Wyatte, variation of Wyatt.

Wycliffe, "village near the cliff," Old English.

Wylie, variation of Wiley.

Wyndham, originally a surname referring to "Wyman's settlement," Old English.

Wynn, Wynne, "friend," Old English.

Wystan, Old English name derived from the words for "battle" and "stone."

X

Xaver, German form of Xavier.

Xavier, "new house," Spanish. First used as a personal name to honor St. Francis Xavier who established the order of the Jesuits.

Xeno, variation of Xenos.

Xenos, "stranger," Greek.

Xerxes, "ruler," Persian. The King of Persia in the fifth century B.C.

Y

Yale, "fertile upland," Welsh.

Yancy, variation of Jan.

Yann, Breton form of John.

Yasir, "rich," Arabic.

Yehudi, Hebrew form of Judah.

Yorath, English form of a Welsh personal name derived from the words for "lord" and "handsome."

Yorick, variation of George.

York, originally a surname referring to a place name. From the Old English word for "yew."

Yosef, original Hebrew form of Joseph.

Yuan, "original," Chinese.

Yul, variation of Julius.

Yuri, Russian form of George.

Yusuf, Arabic form of Joseph.

Yves, French personal name derived from the Old German word for "yew."

Yvon, variation of Yves.

Z

Zac, short form of Zachary or Zachariah.

Zacchaeus, biblical name, possibly from Aramaic, "pure."

Zach, short form of Zachary or Zachariah.

Zachariah, "the Lord has remembered," Hebrew. In the Old Testament, one of the kings of Israel.

Zacharius, variation of Zachariah.

Zachary, variation of Zachariah.

Zack, short form of Zachary or Zachariah.

Zaid, "increase, growth," Arabic.

Zak, short form of Zachary or Zachariah.

Zane, originally a surname, a variation of Shane, from Sean, the Irish Gaelic form of John.

Zavier, variation of Xavier.

Zeb, short form of Zebedee or Zebulun.

Zebedee, biblical name, the Greek form of the Hebrew meaning "gift of Jehovah."

Zebediah, "Jehovah has given," Hebrew.

Zebulun, "exaltation" or "to dwell," Hebrew. An Old Testament name.

Zed, short form of Zedekiah.

Zedekiah, "Jehovah is right," Hebrew.

Zenas, variation of Zeno.

Zeno, "from Zeus," Greek.

Zenobias, "life from Zeus," Greek.

Zeph, short form of Zephaniah, meaning "hidden by God," Hebrew.

Zephan, Zephon, "looking out," Hebrew.

Zilcomo, "thank you," African.